Praise for *Unbossed:*
Are Leading the Way

"*Unbossed* is a celebration of sistas and a field guide for making the world a better place. With wit, verve, love, and wisdom, Khristi Lauren Adams introduces us to eight Black girls with expansive vision and leadership acumen."
—Jemar Tisby, PhD, *New York Times* bestselling author of *The Color of Compromise* and founder of The Witness, Inc.

"Khristi Lauren Adams's *Unbossed* is a bridge that connects the legacy of Black women trailblazers of the past to the Black girls blazing their own trails today. Reading the testimonies of these brilliant young Black leaders, one can only conclude that the kids are all right."
—Ekemini Uwan, public theologian and co-host of the *Truth's Table* podcast

"In *Unbossed*, Khristi Lauren Adams offers us a textbook and a masterclass on Black girls' innate leadership wisdom. Such a gift has never been more important. If you are committed to being a powerful leader, please read this book!"
—Vashti DuBois, executive director of The Colored Girls Museum

"Khristi Lauren Adams's work is truly needed in this moment in time. She has elevated the context of the Black girl's voice, moving us beyond being surprised to acknowledging and embracing the Black girl's voice as genius."
—Vivian Anderson, founder and director of Every Black Girl

"Khristi Lauren Adams has captured what I have always known about Black girls and Black women. We are capable and resilient leaders. We are also vulnerable humans who are in need of love, compassion, tenderness, and support."
—Natasha Sistrunk Robinson, author and president of T3 Leadership Solutions, Inc.

UNBOSSED

UNBOSSED

HOW BLACK GIRLS ARE LEADING THE WAY

KHRISTI LAUREN ADAMS

FOREWORD BY
CHANEQUA WALKER-BARNES

BROADLEAF BOOKS
MINNEAPOLIS

UNBOSSED
How Black Girls Are Leading the Way

Scripture quotations marked (KJV) are from the King James Version.

Scripture quotations marked (NIV) are from the Holy Bible, New International Version®, NIV®. Copyright © 1973, 1978, 1984, 2011 by Biblica, Inc.™ Used by permission of Zondervan. All rights reserved worldwide. www.zondervan.com The "NIV" and "New International Version" are trademarks registered in the United States Patent and Trademark Office by Biblica, Inc.™

Scripture quotations marked (NET) are from the NET Bible® copyright ©1996-2017 by Biblical Studies Press, L.L.C. http://netbible.com All rights reserved.

Photo of Ssanyu Lukoma, chapter 1: Amir Ballard, A. Ballard Creations
Photo of Tyah-Amoy Roberts, chapter 2: Emilee McGovern
Photo of Hannah Lucas, chapter 3: Vania Stoyanova, Vania Photo Studio
Photo of Grace Callwood, chapter 4: NeAnni Y. Ife
Photo of Jaychele Schenck, chapter 5: Aquinnah Crosby
Photo of Amara Ifeji, chapter 6: Phoebe Parker
Photo of Kynnedy Smith, chapter 7: Alvin Smith, The Urban Design Suite
Photo of Stephanie Younger, chapter 8: Emilee McGovern

Cover illustration by Aruna Rangarajan
Cover design by Mighty Media

Print ISBN: 978-1-5064-7426-7
eBook ISBN: 978-1-5064-7427-4

For my sister, Chloe, whose leadership inspires me every single day.

CONTENTS

FOREWORD

In *Unbossed*, Khristi Lauren Adams shows us that for every Black girl genius in the spotlight, there are countless others in the wings. They are artists and activists, innovators and entrepreneurs, organizers and reformers.

The eight girls (some of them now emerging women) featured in *Unbossed* epitomize #blackgirlmagic. They are high achievers who have accomplished successes in their preteen and teen years that even high-achieving adults would be proud to pull off. With widely diverse interests and backgrounds, these girls have one thing in common: they saw a problem, dreamed a solution, and implemented it, often with great odds stacked against them.

In some cases, their own struggles helped them to perceive a need, as Hannah Lucas did when her experiences of bullying, harassment, depression, and suicidality inspired her to develop the notOK mobile app. Likewise, Tyah-Amoy Roberts—a student at Marjory Stoneman Douglas High School at the time of the 2018 campus shooting—stepped up as an activist and spokesperson to challenge the media's exclusion of the Black students who made up 25 percent of the school's population.

In other cases, these girls realized that youth voices and leadership were needed in movements dominated by adults. Stephanie Younger acted on this realization to create the Black Feminist

Collective, an intergenerational platform for womanist and Black feminist thought. Amara Ifeji brings her age, gender, and race to bear as she attempts to bridge the environmental justice and racial justice movements through her organizing, public education, and research. Jaychele Nicole Schenck has realized that as inheritors of the future, young people need to have a bigger role in shaping it. So she started a youth-led social justice movement, Gen Z: We Want to Live.

In every case, these girls recognized their own power to be change agents. Grace Callwood did this when, in the midst of her own cancer treatment, she realized that she had the power to serve other kids who were in foster care or struggling with illness, poverty, or homelessness. Kynnedy Smith did it when she started I Art Cleveland to promote art education in under-resourced communities and again when she started an online forum to promote sisterhood and community among girls and women. Ssanyu Lukoma did it with Brown Kids Read because she saw that kids her age had little exposure to diverse literature.

Each of these girls is a creative visionary who has decided it is never too early to change the world. Their lives are an inspiration to Black girls, women, and anyone else who has been taught that we have to wait our turns, that we are too young, too inexperienced, or too new to lead. One of the gifts of *Unbossed* is Khristi Lauren Adams's deft attention to naming and describing just how these girls embody leadership. Too often, the genius of Black girls and women goes unseen so much that we fail to see it in ourselves. Adams gives us the language for this.

At the same time, Adams refuses readers the temptation we might have to view these young leaders as Strong Black Women-in-the-making, as mythical figures having near superhuman capacities for fixing things. Adams shows us their strength and resilience, to be sure. But she also opens a window to their vulnerabilities: serious illness, financial instability, depression, anxiety, lack of support from teachers, loneliness, insecurity, and struggles with body shaming and colorism. Adams shows us that being exceptional does not render them immune from the hardships of Black girlhood. They may accomplish seemingly magical things at times, but they are neither magical nor mythical themselves.

They are ordinary girls who reach for the extraordinary—and who inspire the rest of us to do likewise.

—Dr. Chanequa Walker-Barnes, author of *I Bring the Voices of My People* and *Too Heavy a Yoke*

INTRODUCTION

On January 20, 2021, Amanda Gorman stepped to the podium with poise and confidence. In a commanding voice that served the magnitude of the moment, the National Youth Poet Laureate captured the nation's attention with her inaugural poem, "The Hill We Climb." In the moments following, news media outlets marveled at the young poet and activist. "How is she only twenty-two?" one reporter asked. "She reminds me of Maya Angelou," another journalist said. "She's a young hero!" another exclaimed. It's as if her presence, her maturity, and her wisdom came as a surprise.

Yet the brilliance of this young poet was not unforeseen. The very presence of Vice President Kamala Harris and former first lady Michelle Obama at that ceremony should have left no room for surprise. Of course an Amanda Gorman exists! Both Vice President Harris and Michelle Obama were once twenty-two-year-old leaders like Gorman herself.

In some ways, the surprise itself was telling. *Why* were so many people seemingly surprised by a Black girl's brilliance, leadership, and confidence? Black women and girls have demonstrated their leadership to this world for as long as we have existed. Claudette Colvin was only fifteen years old when she refused to give up her seat to a white woman on a segregated bus in 1955. Sixteen-year-old Barbara Johns led her classmates in a strike to protest the substandard conditions at her high school in Prince Edward County, Virginia, in 1961. Nine-year-old Audrey Faye Hendricks was the youngest marcher arrested for a civil rights protest in Birmingham, Alabama, in 1963.

And notably, a twenty-two-year-old college student named Praithia Hall spoke at a church meeting in Terrell County, Georgia, in 1962, where Martin Luther King Jr. would be in attendance. At that meeting, she uttered the phrase "I have a dream" repeatedly in a prayer, sharing her vision for Black people in America. King would later express his admiration for her oratorical skills, and he was, of course, particularly impressed with the phrase "I have a dream." We would go on to hear Hall's influence expressed in King's now famous speech at the 1963 March on Washington for Jobs and Freedom.

In 1972, Shirley Chisholm became the first woman and first Black major-party candidate to run for president of the United States. Her campaign message was "Unbought & Unbossed," which became the title of her memoir. Today, almost fifty years later, young Black girls are following in her legacy with their leadership, resilience, and integrity. They, too, are showing the world that they are unbossed: unapologetic in their calling and approach to leading on their own terms.

Though their stories are often overlooked, Black girls have always played important roles in social movements in the fight for a better and more equal world. Young Black people played a pivotal role at the height of these movements, and we often call to mind their activism and the lessons they have taught us. In the same way we learned from the Black youth of previous generations, we must turn our attention to the lives of rising Black girl leaders of today. It is important to pay attention to their leadership now because their passion, strength of character, and vision will teach and inspire us in this ever-changing world.

Growing up as a Black girl, I found that leadership came naturally to me. Yet I had difficulty reconciling my innate gift with the shame, insecurity, and invisibility that society imposed due to my race and gender. These struggles took years to overcome, yet I was able to evolve as a leader despite these obstacles. My professional career has included more than fifteen years of experience in education, ministry, and counseling. In many of those arenas I have been either the first woman, the first woman of color, or the first Black woman holding a position of authority. This has made me fully aware of the responsibility I have to the Black girls who see me in those positions. I understand the importance of representation for them, and how essential it is to leverage my resources to create safe spaces for their leadership to blossom. In the encounters and relationships I have developed with Black girls, I have learned much from their wisdom and resilience.

My first book, *Parable of the Brown Girl: The Sacred Lives of Girls of Color*, focuses on narratives of personal encounters I have had with Black girls and the truths that emerged through the girls' stories and wisdom. Now in *Unbossed: How Black Girls Are Leading the Way*, I introduce young Black leaders whom most of mainstream society has not met but whose exceptional leadership is substantive enough to educate us all—youth and adults—on the multidisciplinary field of leadership. Each chapter introduces one of eight young women and her work and includes a brief analysis of her specific leadership style. I explore how these girls are connected to Black women leaders who have gone before them, and highlight the leadership wisdom that each girl demonstrates and that I believe offers universal truths for readers.

In her book *Black Women as Leaders*, Lori Latrice Martin writes, "The importance of creating a perspective on the practice of leadership that is black women–centered cannot be understated. Much of the literature on leadership theory is white men–centered. Thus, leadership theory requires new ways of theorizing leadership and changing dominant narratives about leadership."

Black girl leaders have emerged from the margins to be the voice of change. The eight Black girls featured in this book are the Black women we will be reading about and studying for decades to come. We must take heed of the wisdom of their leadership. Black girls like Amanda Gorman have given us a glimpse of what's ahead. Maybe we'll be less surprised by Black girls' brilliance as we become more aware of how it surrounds us all the time. The future toward which we look will be led by Black women and girls.

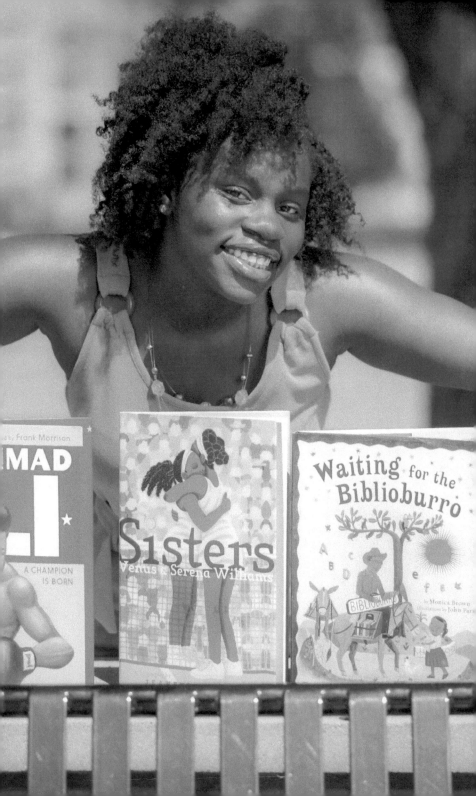

BORN WITH PURPOSE
THE STRATEGIC THINKING OF SSANYU LUKOMA

*I want to make Brown Kids Read a big thing to
show kids that a Black girl can do this and that
Black girls are important enough to be featured in literature.*
—Ssanyu Lukoma, founder of Brown Kids Read

W hen she was just five years old, Ssanyu Lukoma fell in love
with a book called *Rosa*, an inspiring children's book about
Rosa Parks written by poet, activist, and educator Nikki Giovanni.
The children's picture book recounts the day Rosa Parks refused
to give up her seat for a white person on a segregated bus and
describes how this launched the famous 1955 Montgomery Bus
Boycott. The book gives background into Rosa Parks's life and

activism, as well as highlighting other women who made the movement possible.

"I was so in love with the story because I like to imagine that, if I were in Rosa's position, I would make the same decision that she did," Ssanyu says. Well into her teenage years, Ssanyu still has the book that made such an impact on her as a young girl. "I want to give it to my kids when I grow up, because I love that book so much."

In December 2008, Ssanyu was three years old and rehearsing with the choir at her church. "But I wasn't allowed to have a lyric sheet because only the big kids who could read were allowed to have one," Ssanyu remembers. She was so disappointed that she determined that something would change. "We left for the holiday break, and I wanted to read so badly. So by the time we came back to choir in late January, I had learned how to read enough so that I could have a lyric sheet." Over the span of six or seven weeks, she had taught herself to read. By that time Ssanyu had turned four. "Everyone in the choir was shocked and impressed," she says with a smile. "That was the first time my mother knew that I was going to be an extremely avid reader." Ever since then, she has had a passion for words and reading. "Not all readers are leaders, but all leaders are readers," Harry S. Truman once said. In Ssanyu's case, a passion for reading was the foundation of leadership.

I was first introduced to Ssanyu when a friend suggested I partner with a local organization for an event for my first book, *Parable of the Brown Girl*. The event was to be held at a local bookstore, and we decided that raising money for a nonprofit run by a young Black woman would help push our agenda of supporting Black girls. Besides, my friend told me, that way I'd get to connect to the founder of Brown Kids Read. "You just have to meet this young lady. She is sharp," my friend said.

Ssanyu was just fourteen years old when we first met in a Starbucks on a cold fall day. I loved her immediately. She is witty and vibrant, with a bright and energetic smile. Ssanyu is the very embodiment of her name, which means "joy" or "gladness" and is of African Luganda origin. Ssanyu has a joyous and energetic persona. "I think that once somebody meets me, they can kind of get a feel for my personality," she tells me. "A lot of people can tell I like to talk a lot and they can also tell I have a lot of high energy or I can be bossy at times. And it's not like I try and hide those things!"

She is very comfortable around adults, and I felt as though we had known each other for years. In a short amount of time, she told me more about herself and what she does in her free time.

Ssanyu loves being a homeschooled student because she enjoys the freedom and flexibility that comes with it. At the same time, she is a very social person and misses being with her friends during the school day. Her favorite subject is literature or anything having to do with reading and writing. "Books create so many pathways," she says. Ssanyu is a proud member of two organizations in addition to her own nonprofit: NJ Orators, through which she does competitive public speaking, and KiDz HuB Media Network, an organization that trains and mentors youth as junior broadcasters and journalists.

After some small talk, Ssanyu dove into her assessment of my book *Parable of the Brown Girl* and expressed appreciation for how she felt it represented her in some important ways. I was surprised. I didn't expect her to have read the book and was flattered that she would have taken the time to read and share her thoughts.

Then again, Ssanyu strikes me as someone who never comes to a meeting unprepared. While we were there for what was essentially a business meeting—figuring out a partnership between her nonprofit and my book launch—her infectious personality made me want to know more about her and, more specifically, what motivates her.

Ssanyu is the proud older sister to her young brother and sister. She works to better herself as a leader for them first. "They look up to me a lot," she says about her siblings. "When I do different things, I want to make sure I am a good role model for them to look up to."

Ssanyu fears for her siblings' safety. In an era in which mass shootings are on the rise and violent white supremacy is at work, she worries. "All the things going on, like school shootings and Black men being killed in the street—it hurts," she says with concern. "I get scared. My little brother is nine. I don't want him to walk outside and be scared that he's going to be holding a bag of candy and somebody is going to come and attack him just because of the color of his skin."

For comfort and strength, Ssanyu turns to her faith in God. Ever since she was young, she and her family have been very active in her local church. "I feel like God placed me in that environment so that I was able to feel like nothing can stop me," she says. In her words I hear her gratitude for the love and care and support of her church community. She sees God in the relationships she has been able to build there. "In Sunday school, we were just studying the Scripture 'For I know the plans I have for you, . . . plans to prosper you and not to harm you, plans to give you hope and a future' [Jeremiah 29:11 NIV]. That really touched me," she says. "When I feel like I want to give up, I know that it hurts God when I have those thoughts because he gave me talent and he gave me gifts and he gave me a special purpose to do these things. And that's why I keep pushing and I keep going."

This persistence—and her commitment to use the gifts God has given her—has propelled Ssanyu to one of her greatest achievements: founding the organization Brown Kids Read. It's an idea she thought of when she was just twelve years old.

Brown Kids Read

"The first time I thought of Brown Kids Read, it wasn't supposed to be an organization," she recalls. "It was just supposed to be a partnership with another nonprofit to do a fundraiser for them."

The nonprofit, Double Dose, was led by Ssanyu's friends, a set of twins who wrote a book together. At the time, Ssanyu was working with another author to turn her book into a party entertainment business. When Ssanyu heard that Double Dose was doing an event at Barnes and Noble, she pitched an idea to the twins: connecting their book launch with the party entertainment idea.

"We needed a name for it, since Barnes and Noble asks for the name of your event. So we came up with Brown Kids Read. Once I got to that event and I saw the kids buying the books and I saw the excitement on their faces, I was like, 'I want to replicate this.'"

Ssanyu realized that a lot of the kids in her age group did not have the opportunity to read and learn about diverse literature. "My parents made an effort to give me books that portrayed Black women as strong and confident," she says. "I grew up having a lot of diverse books. I grew up with a bookshelf full of books featuring people who looked like me. But several of my peers and friends didn't have that opportunity. So I wanted to make sure that the next generation did not have that lack of diverse books. I wanted to make sure that they had access to them, which is very important."

Ssanyu's thoughts run parallel to a wider movement from We Need Diverse Books (WNDB), called #OwnVoices based on a hashtag that started on Twitter and by which people recommended books about diverse characters written by authors who are themselves from marginalized identities. The movement highlights the importance of representation by diverse authors. The hashtag started by calling attention to diversity in children's literature, but it has since expanded to all literature. Alaina Leary, a Boston-based publishing professional, wrote about the importance of the #OwnVoices movement: "The reason that #OwnVoices creators are so important is because, as marginalized people, we're the best authority on telling our own stories. It's great that more people are talking about how to write authentic, sensitive stories outside their experience, and getting sensitivity readers involved, but it's also important that marginalized people are able to tell their own stories." (WNDB recently decided to discontinue using the #OwnVoices hashtag and instead will use specific descriptions that authors use for themselves and their characters.)

Ssanyu picked up on the same need for diverse literature before she knew anything about the Own Voices movement. She is intuitive—able to see the need for such books on her own. This is significant because it demonstrates that Black youth are not only aware of the lack of representation in literature; they are proactive in the solutions.

In an effort to make Brown Kids Read more marketable and appealing to kids, Ssanyu built on the concept of bringing books to life. The organization's nonprofit status became official in November 2018. By the beginning of 2019, Ssanyu, with the help of her mother and father, had put on a series of community reading events, which exposed youth to new literature and at which local authors read excerpts and held giveaways. She eventually realized how difficult it is to get kids out on Saturdays to read. Weekends are the days that youth have off from school, and thus, anything resembling academics was a turnoff to some. Ssanyu was also competing against weekend commitments like sports and other extracurriculars. While this frustrated Ssanyu, she was determined to find a creative way to move forward. She came up with the concept of a pop-up bookstore: a traveling book display that she could take to local events. Her parents loaned her $2,000 to purchase books, and she began setting up the Brown Kids Read pop-up bookstore to display and sell books at various events. "That was another way to get kids excited," she says. "They got to see a whole bunch of books with people that are featuring them and people who are from other countries and people that they didn't know about."

From there, the Brown Kids Read social media reach began to grow, and organizations began to contact Ssanyu for interviews, to support her work, and to get the word out about the organization. Brown Kids Read now offers a host of events throughout the year. Ssanyu continues to promote the importance of diverse books for youth through various Brown Kids Read initiatives, such as a book club for teenagers called Book Junkie Insider, in which teens "discuss relevant and thought-provoking books with an action plan in mind." Ssanyu recently started the *Book Junkie* podcast, in which she converses with her friends and peers about young adult books. The website Brown Kids Read sells merchandise such as tote bags, journals, T-shirts, and travel mugs. Ssanyu also offers book reviews for the diverse literature she promotes, and shares her contagious love for books with her readers. In one review she writes, "When I began to read

Slay, it felt like a mixture of *The Hunger Games* and *The Hate U Give* (both books I strongly recommend). I loved the concept and story because it's uncommon to find black girls as main characters in Young Adult literature that are strong individuals and painted in a positive light." The organization also offers young people the opportunity to read and review books of their choosing on the site. And from time to time, Brown Kids Read offers essay-writing contests for youth, with the opportunity to win cash prizes and other gifts.

Along with these initiatives, the Brown Kids Read website offers books for sale. The site's main page features a diverse array of illustrated brown faces on the covers. Above the books is a picture of Ssanyu, beaming with pride, her arms stretched wide to show the display of books.

Though lighthearted in nature, Ssanyu is very serious about the work she does and the young people she serves through her organization. Ssanyu has said time and time again that she wants the kids she serves to be excited: she wants them to be excited about books, and she believes that representation of diverse voices is the gateway to that excitement.

"I want to make Brown Kids Read a big thing to show kids that a Black girl can do this and that Black girls are important enough to be featured in literature," she says. "Reading can be a great form of entertainment, and you can learn from it at the same time."

Through Brown Kids Read, Ssanyu motivates young people to read books that feature children of color. She believes that by making reading fun and relatable, she can share her love of literature and inspire the next generation of readers. "God gave me purpose," she says simply. "My purpose is to lead. My purpose is to inspire people."

Strategic Leadership

Ssanyu Lukoma is a problem-solver. She prides herself on her ability to think critically. She reflects on all her endeavors, thinking about what she can do better the next time. Any time she has had challenges, she considers them teachable moments. "I am very good at seeing the logic in situations," she says when I ask her to describe her leadership style. "I'm always trying to figure out what's the most efficient way to do something or how we can solve a problem quickly."

Ssanyu is a strategic leader: she has a goal in mind and enacts a careful and intentional plan in order to get to that goal. Ssanyu's vision for Brown Kids Read is based on the female Black leaders she read about as a child; she in turn wants to make a difference by inspiring others. "I read about people like Rosa Parks, Katherine Johnson, and Ruby Bridges, who all inspired me to be like them—a world-changing female. I want to make a difference by inspiring kids to choose more diverse literature and making those books accessible to them." According to Management Study Guide, an educational portal for students and corporations, strategic leadership refers to "a manager's potential to express a strategic vision for the organization . . . and to motivate and persuade others to acquire that vision." Strategic leaders create structures to equip their organization to achieve its goals, and Ssanyu did just that. She created a structure for Brown Kids Read that will maximize the organization's ability to reach as many youth as possible and to expose them to diverse literature. She has created different avenues to do this, including community events, podcasts, book reviews, and other means.

But Ssanyu's strategic leadership is not limited to these initial strategies. Strategic leaders consistently think about their organization's long-term success while also keeping their focus on short-term stability. She is constantly reevaluating where her organization is and thinking up new processes and action plans to move toward the Brown Kids Read vision. Her innate strategic skills align with the organization strategy process that Hughes, Beatty, and Dinwoodie outline in their book, *Becoming a Strategic Leader: Your Role in Your Organization's Enduring Success*: the strategic leader sets a mission and values, creates a strategy, executes the strategy, and then assesses. This is Ssanyu's ongoing leadership approach. It is a purposeful process of continual improvement for both the organization and herself.

The Strategic Moral Leadership of Black Women

One significant aspect of Ssanyu's strategic approach is that her leadership is rooted in a sense of moral obligation. In her case, that ethical obligation is to fulfill what she believes is the call God placed on her life. "Why would God give me this if I was just supposed to give up?" she asks.

This belief—that strategic leadership emerges from moral obligation—is rooted in a history of Black women who connect their religious and spiritual duties to their social responsibilities. In her book *Witnessing and Testifying: Black Women, Religion, and Civil Rights*, Rosetta E. Ross writes, "The 'obligation' to contribute to improving social life as 'earning your space in the world' originated in response to the particular circumstances of African-Americans. Black women understand this value as responsibility." In order to fulfill this responsibility, states Ross, Black women look to determine the best response to those social needs.

For Ssanyu, fulfilling her moral obligation means using the gifts God gave her to address a pressing social need: brown children finally seeing themselves represented in literature. Ross presents four themes of responsibility among Black religious women:

"(1) responsibility to practice and pass on particular virtues that attend to surviving and thriving as persons, (2) responsibility to work in partnership with God for community survival and positive quality of life, (3) responsibility to attend [to the] needs of the least, and (4) responsibility to participate in community-building and community-sustaining practices."

Ssanyu's entrepreneurial pursuits are centered on these themes and can be viewed as a call-and-response. A call-and-response is an interaction between a speaker and their listeners: one calls and the other responds. Ssanyu believes that God has called her to the work that she does. Her response is to responsibly use her gifts and pass on virtues of character, commitment, and compassion to those who follow, like her siblings and the young people she serves. She believes she is doing God's work for the betterment and survival of the Black community. She responsibly tends to the needs of young minority children who rarely see themselves represented in literature, and she participates in the community-building and community-sustaining practices of service.

Rosetta Ross writes about Black women in history who, similar to Ssanyu, practiced social responsibility as a means of fulfilling a duty to God. Victoria Way DeLee, a grassroots community activist who saw her calling to civil rights work as God's work, is one of many foremothers to Ssanyu. DeLee spent much of her early childhood active in her local church, attending with her grandmother, and Ross writes that her church experiences, alongside her faith in God, were an integral part of her self-understanding.

While DeLee struggled to reconcile the treatment and conditions of African Americans that she witnessed firsthand, the values she learned in church allowed her to turn away from vengeance or retribution and instead to focus her energy on justice. Her immediate concern was changing conditions for those within her own community, and she focused her efforts on voting rights, boycotts, and community-wide efforts to desegregate schools. "DeLee worked to improve people's lives by seeking justice in her local community as a means of serving God," writes Ross.

Ssanyu's upbringing in the church and her sense of moral obligation have resulted in a worldview similar to DeLee's. "I was born and raised in the church. I used to spend so much time there, I'm telling you!" she says. "I would have public speaking, dance, choir, and church on Sunday. I was surrounded by my church family, who have always supported me. It makes me feel like I have nothing to be afraid of." Like DeLee's work, Ssanyu's efforts tend to the needs of her community. Listening to Ssanyu talk to teenagers via her podcast about the importance of voting, you can even see a resemblance to DeLee's pursuits. The Black girl leaders of our present and future have clearly inherited the lifeblood of the Black female leaders of our past.

Ssanyu's Leadership Wisdom

Ssanyu's strategic leadership offers lessons for the rest of us. Following are just a few of the beliefs undergirding her style.

You Have to Work for It

As a young woman of faith, Ssanyu believes that her faith must be supported by work. There is a Scripture passage that says that faith unaccompanied by action is useless (James 2:17). Ssanyu's good deeds are a product of her faith. "God is never going to just hand things to you," she says. "You have to work for it. If you just give up, then what is that saying to God? That you're not going to use the talent that he gave you? We have a purpose in being here." To Ssanyu, it is not enough to have talent; we must use our gifts and work for the goals we seek to attain and in faithful response to God.

I spent my first year of college researching various groups on campus and figuring out which ones I wanted to join. I recall being frustrated because I could not find a group that fit who I was. Months went by, during which I went to class and spent time with friends and studied. But I felt like something was missing. I'd complain to friends that I did not feel like I was using my gifts.

One day a mentor said to me, "If you can't find it, then start it." Those simple words moved me; they helped me travel from one place in my mind to another. I went from being discouraged by what I could not find in others to being encouraged by what I could find within myself. I called together a group of friends, and we brainstormed what the needs of the campus and community were and how we could meet them. Within a few weeks, we had a plan and an application submitted to the Student Activities Office to start our own campus organization.

Our newly founded organization did both creative work and service projects to meet needs of our community both on and off campus. By the end of my senior year, we received an award for being the most active organization on campus. Our group had its fair share of growing pains and challenges as we sought to figure out the best way we could be of use. But when I look back on that time in my life, I can say with confidence that we put our faith into action. What I had been seeking when I got to college was in me all along. But like Ssanyu says, God did not just hand us the organization; we had to work for it.

Our culture highlights instant success. Someone's tweet or video that goes viral, the person walking through a store who is discovered by a talent agent—success stories like these are not a reality for the majority. For many of us, a commitment to working hard will garner results. At the same time, hard work is by no means a formula for success. Sometimes our hard work won't produce the results we want. However, working hard gives us the opportunity to exercise our gifts and talents. Working hard allows us to put them to good use in this world. That alone is reason enough to be diligent.

Do What You Have Passion For

In an interview with the website Kebloom, which helps young entrepreneurs launch ideas and services, Ssanyu says, "Some advice I have for other entrepreneurs is, do not do it for the money. I know that a lot of teenagers will want to start a business just to make money. Brown Kids Read is something I really have a passion for. I love reading, I love business, I love making things come to life, and that's why I created Brown Kids Read." Doing work that we love—regardless of the income it produces and whether it ever becomes our career—is key to fulfillment.

When I was a teenager, someone asked me, "If you could do anything in the world and you never had to worry about money, what would it be?" Although my career has taken me to different contexts, one thing that remains consistent is my commitment to working as an advocate for young Black girls. Empowering Black girls is my passion. I am passionate about other things as well, but advocating for young Black women is the passion that has informed my life's work.

Some people have a difficult time discovering what they are passionate about. Ask yourself the question that was asked to me as a young girl: "If you could do anything in the world and you never had to worry about money, what would it be?" With Ssanyu, success is not only about making money, although she ultimately wants to run a thriving business. Ssanyu believes that her passion will drive that success. Her passion is her primary motivating factor.

That said, the energy, effort, and time required to focus on our passions can ultimately lead to burnout if we are not careful. Without proper self-care, we might find that even the things we're passionate about can cause stress and exhaustion. Sometimes Ssanyu has to step away from her business in order to care for herself.

"Basketball!" she exclaims, when I ask her what she does to decompress. "It's one of the ways that I can refocus myself. Even when I hit a roadblock for Brown Kids Read, I'll go outside to my basketball hoop and shoot a couple hundred foul shots."

Reading books, apart from her business endeavors, also happens to be Ssanyu's self-care. She says she reads when she's stressed because through a book, she is "taken to another world." Ssanyu demonstrates that we must create a practical harmony between the commitment to our passions and our well-being.

We Each Have a Special Purpose

People like Ssanyu make sense of the world around them by finding growth and meaning in their environments. A philosophical concept called "being-in-the-world" emphasizes this idea: that each individual navigates their life in unique ways.

For example, Ssanyu's being-in-the-world is reflected in how she practices community work as a moral value. It is how she embodies what she deems to be her unique purpose. Each of us has a purpose that distinctly reflects who God created us to be. We can discover that purpose through the things we're passionate about and through our gifts and talents. We can also discover our purpose through our own personal story, our background, and our experiences.

No matter how we discern our purpose, I truly believe that like Ssanyu, we all have specific contributions to make to the world. Ssanyu's beliefs about her purpose are embodied by how she moves through the world.

Born with Purpose

Fans of Brown Kids Read will be happy to hear of Ssanyu's book-in-progress. "Every time I do an event or go somewhere people are like, 'Okay, you're selling books, but where is *your* book?'" Ssanyu tells me.

In the summer of 2020, Ssanyu got an idea for a children's book. "This is a rough title, but it's called *Suubi's Sunny Smile*. It's my brother's middle name." The story is about a little boy who doesn't like to read. He wants to be an astronaut when he grows up, or someone who goes on adventures. His teacher gives him an assignment to find a book to read. He does so, reluctantly. One day, however, Suubi finds a book that he loves that incorporates all the things he likes doing in real life. He comes to realize that books can take him to another whole world.

Ssanyu has written the first draft, and now she's debating whether to self-publish or pitch the book to a publisher. One day, perhaps, Ssanyu won't have to worry about this question at all; her long-term goals include expanding Brown Kids Read into a publishing company. "And to not only become a publishing company, but to have those personal relationships with the authors, bring events to schools," she says—similar to what Scholastic Book Fairs offer but with a continued emphasis on Black and brown readers and writers.

Ssanyu wants to take advantage of all possible avenues for Brown Kids Read. New ideas for programs and events come to her almost daily. "There's another project that I want to do called the Brown Kids Read Book Bus," she tells me, "kind of like a traveling bookstore that we can drive to different schools."

Ssanyu is the same driven, determined young woman I met in that Starbucks several years ago. She has multifaceted aspirations for her future. She wants to act, have her own talk show, and be a producer. Ssanyu is confident that there are many different avenues she could pursue, but right now she feels she is on a path similar to the global media leader, philanthropist, producer, and actress Oprah Winfrey.

"When I was younger, Oprah Winfrey was the first strong Black woman that I saw, other than my mother, who was the epitome of what I wanted to be," she tells me. "Now people are telling me that I'm going to be the next Oprah."

But Ssanyu balks at the thought of becoming the "next" anything. "I've come to the realization that I don't want to be the next Oprah," she says with a smile. "I want to be the first Ssanyu."

2

MARCHING FOR BLACK LIVES
THE TRANSFORMING ACTIVISM OF TYAH-AMOY ROBERTS

I feel like Black women are literally the helm of every movement.
Every push for social justice. Every push for social change.
We need to take our stories into our own hands.
–Tyah-Amoy Roberts, activist, speaker, and student organizer

❧

■■ There was just a shooting at your high school."

Tyah-Amoy Roberts looked down in disbelief at the text message from her mother. It had only been a few minutes since her mom had dropped her off at a local community college to attend a class—part of an accelerated program for high school students. At first, Tyah disregarded the message, thinking her mother had gotten the wrong information and it was just a drill.

Still, something told her to look online to see if it was true. It was.

On February 14, 2018, a gunman opened fire with a semiautomatic rifle at Marjory Stoneman Douglas High School (MSD) in Parkland, Florida. Claiming the lives of seventeen people and injuring seventeen others, it was one of the deadliest school shootings in United States history.

At the time, Tyah was a junior at the school. She had left the building less than twenty minutes before the shooting occurred. While she was not physically on campus at the time, the emotional devastation left her feeling helpless. "I was calling my friends and they weren't answering, and I was so scared," she recalls now, with difficulty. "I was soaked in tears so much that my dress was messed up."

That day in her class at the community college, Tyah was scheduled to give a speech. Aware of the tragedy taking place at MSD, her teacher told her she could be excused. "I was like 'No, I'm going to give the speech,'" Tyah reflects now—a decision that foreshadowed how she would later channel her pain from the tragedy into transformative speaking. But meanwhile, Tyah wasn't sure how to process what was happening. She felt a lot of internal tension: relief that she was not at the school at the time; shame about not being with her friends and classmates. She still has a hard time talking about that day because it calls forth such pain.

"It was a traumatic experience," she tells me. "I don't even remember a lot about that day."

In the days and weeks that followed, Tyah attended funeral after funeral for her classmates while still going to school and trying to move forward with the rest of her peers. She had a difficult time processing what had taken place. "After that day, it was kind of just me pretending that it didn't happen."

March for Our Lives

Tyah is now a sophomore at Stanford University. "It feels like it was twenty years ago," she tells me, because so much has occurred in the years since the shooting. Tyah speaks introspectively about the events of the intervening years, as if she is discovering different parts of herself through the retelling. There is no doubt that her whole life was transformed by what happened on February 14, 2018. Yet she has reached through the depths of pain and emerged as a voice for change.

Initially after the shooting, national attention focused heavily on the school and the surviving students. Some survivors sought counseling and formed support groups. Some found comfort in trying to return to what remained of life, snatching whatever sense of normalcy they could by spending time with friends and attending classes. Others turned their grief and anger into activism.

A little over a month after the tragedy, *Time* magazine did a cover story on five survivor-activists at the forefront of the gun-control conversation: Jaclyn Corin, Emma González, David Hogg, Cameron Kasky, and Alex Wind. They rapidly became, to the public, the faces of the Marjory Stoneman Douglas High School survivors.

Those faces, however, were noticeably white (though González's father is Cuban). At the time, MSD was about 25 percent Black, yet outsiders would not have known that based on the media's depictions of the school.

A few weeks after the shooting, Tyah's friend and classmate Mei-Ling called her, wanting to talk through her frustrations about the way the media was ignoring the Black students who were speaking out against gun violence as well. During that conversation, the two decided to host a press conference about feeling silenced as members of the Stoneman Douglas Black student community. The press conference happened to be just a few days after the March for Our Lives rally in Washington, DC, a student-led demonstration to bring attention to gun violence and promote gun-prevention legislation. A school board member had helped the Black high school students get in touch with the local news media and other important members of the community.

I remember seeing this group of students on television at the time and wondering why they had been ignored. In the press conference, Tyah spoke passionately in front of members of the media and alongside other Black students from MSD.

"I am here today with my classmates because we have been sorely underrepresented, and in some cases, misrepresented," she said to the press. "The Black Lives Matter movement has been addressing this topic since the murder of Trayvon Martin in 2012, yet we have never seen this kind of support for our cause, and we surely do not feel that the lives or voices of minorities are valued as much as those of our white counterparts."

"We talked about feeling marginalized, and how this is not a unique experience for Black students," Tyah tells me. "Obviously there's the intersection between gun violence that happens in schools in suburban neighborhoods and gun violence that happens in Black communities. And obviously one gets more attention."

After that initial press conference, Tyah and the group began making contact with schools in predominantly Black communities to offer support. "We essentially formed a coalition," she explains, "because we wanted to make sure that [what would become the organization] March for Our Lives would share their resources with organizations in Black communities in other parts of Broward County that didn't necessarily have the same access to news outlets and money that we had in Parkland."

As time went on, Tyah got more involved in speaking engagements and panels, where people were surprised to see a young Black student. "They were like, 'I didn't know there were Black kids at Douglas!'" Tyah recalls. "At that point, I thought, 'Maybe there does need to be a voice. Maybe there needs to be someone speaking for the Black Stoneman Douglas population.'"

Tyah wasn't sure if she should be that person, but she felt herself getting angrier at how the Black students continued to be overlooked. Her main point of contention was that some of those newly popular student-activists were now turning their public attention to supporting Black students in areas like Washington, DC, and Chicago—yet they weren't looking to the Black students at their very own school to help support their efforts.

"I was feeling mad. And what do millennials and Gen Zers do when they get upset?" Tyah says. "They take to Twitter!" She and I share a laugh.

Tyah communicated with one of those student-activists publicly on Twitter, saying that they see each other in school every day and she wanted to know why they weren't speaking to her on these issues. Shortly after that, Emma González—though not the recipient of the original tweet—texted her and asked if she wanted to go on a "Road for Change" trip with them. Road for Change was an extension of March for Our Lives, during which the group of young activists would make stops on a tour across America to get young people registered and motivated to vote.

The summer before her senior year of high school, Tyah traveled with the other students. She looks back on the experience as both exciting and difficult, and as a time during which she matured a lot, in part because she was away from her parents. Tyah sat on panels, but she gave a lot of speeches as well, which she enjoyed doing. Because of her strong communication skills, March for Our Lives kept her on as a speaker, and she began flying all over the country to speak at various events. Her speeches usually veered away from recounting the specifics of the school shooting and instead reminded audiences of the need to support Black communities.

The busy speaking schedule continued for most of Tyah's senior year, which caused her to struggle as she juggled travel with schoolwork. "To this day I don't know how I did it," Tyah says, shaking her head. "I would be up finishing my homework at two a.m. and then was like, 'Before I go to sleep, I've got to spend another hour writing a speech.' Then I would go to bed at three a.m. and have to wake up at six."

By the end of her senior year, Tyah was a board member for March for Our Lives. At the same time, she was working two jobs to save up money for college and had become an ambassador for the United State of Women, a national organization dedicated "to convening, connecting, and amplifying voices in the fight for full gender equity." Tyah worked primarily on the issue of equity for women of color. She also worked with the Brady Campaign to Prevent Gun Violence, an organization named after Jim and Sarah Brady, who dedicated their lives to advocating for common-sense gun laws at the state and federal level.

During Tyah's first few months at Stanford, she continued to stay busy with her responsibilities for March for Our Lives. Eventually, however, she stepped back from some of her organizational duties to focus on schoolwork. Tyah also wanted to explore more of the university and engage the school's Black community. At the same time, she has no intention of leaving her activist work behind and continues to stay abreast of the happenings related to March for Our Lives.

Currently, there are March for Our Lives chapters all over the world. Tyah is proud of the organization's breadth and spread, though her work has been specific. "I spent my year as a board member trying to diversify the chapters," she says. "How do you have an all-white chapter in Chicago? Like, how does that happen? It's because of what March represents fundamentally and how everybody views it: they view it as a white organization because that's who you guys [March leaders] use the most and that's who you guys capitalize on and highlight. If you want Black people to join the organization, then you have to highlight Black stories. You have to care about Black lives, actively."

Tyah-Amoy Roberts is a contemporary model of transformational leadership that challenges, inspires, and motivates. In her work, she asks her counterparts: What kind of a society are you creating by means of your philosophies and actions? How are you incorporating the voices of the marginalized through your work? Tyah adamantly rejects any vision of a society that excludes Black leadership and livelihood.

Transforming Leadership

Transformational leadership changes people by holding individuals to a high ethical and moral standard: the transformation that happens is a result of individuals being inspired to achieve collective goals. The concept of transformational leadership was first theorized by James MacGregor Burns in his 1978 writings on political leadership. Nancy C. Roberts writes, "Enacted in its authentic form, transformational leadership enhances the motivation, morale and performance of followers through a variety of mechanisms. These include connecting the follower's sense of identity and self to the mission and the collective identity of the organization; being a role model for followers that inspires them."

Transformational leaders like Tyah engage with others and create connection through influence and inspiration. Such leadership energizes and motivates people, inspiring them toward a shared vision. Burns referred to this kind of leadership as "moral leadership," suggesting that it can produce social change through its emphasis on instilling hope and purpose. Transformational leadership focuses on liberty, justice, and equality. It is typically embodied by a charismatic and visionary leader who connects the identity of the people with a larger mission.

In her book *Transformative Leadership*, Carolyn M. Shields lists the basic tenets of transformative leadership—traits that are unmistakable when you observe Tyah's leadership style. First, Shields writes that *transformational leaders acknowledge power and privilege*. Tyah has consistently called out the role that power and privilege played in the lack of attention on the Black student voices calling for gun control at MSD. The frustration she and her peers displayed during their press conference shed light not only on the Black students at their own school but also on those in disadvantaged communities that lack the resources or media attention. Tyah was able to draw attention to practices that uphold privilege and power. She recognizes the role power and privilege played not only externally but personally as well. "Even as marginalized as I am as a Black, queer woman, I still use my privilege to step up and step back for others," she explains. "Almost everyone on this planet has a position of privilege in some way. Knowing how to use that to the advantage of people that don't have that same privilege is one of the most important things I've ever had to learn in life."

The second tenet of transformational leadership that Tyah enacts is that *transformational leaders deconstruct frameworks that generate inequity and then reconstruct them.* Tyah challenged a social-activist framework that was emerging from the Parkland tragedy that excluded Black voices from the national conversation on gun control. She spoke out against any national conversations on gun-violence prevention that did not extend to the Black community as well. Overlapping with that tenet is the idea that *transformational leaders effect deep and equitable change.* She was committed to pushing the national conversation, through the March for Our Lives organization, to focus on Black communities. As a result of Tyah's leadership, the March for Our Lives activists crossed racial barriers through their intentional engagement with issues that affect communities of color. March for Our Lives as an organization continues its commitment to supporting Black communities and partnering with other organizations dedicated to stopping anti-Black violence.

The final example of truth that Tyah embodies is that *transformational leaders demonstrate moral change and activism.* Tyah's courageous activism has helped bring about awareness and change both politically and socially. Her leadership has caused many to take inventory of their own moral principles and how those principles may have contributed to the problems in our society. The presence of student-activists like Tyah challenges us to confront the painful realities of what kind of society we have become. These students reveal that we have become complacent and averse to change. They show us that perhaps we have strayed

33

from our values and ethics. They are fighting for a better society in areas where we as adults should be protecting them and fighting in their place.

Black Women as Transformative Leaders

"Black women are literally [at] the helm of every movement," Tyah says. "Every push for social justice. Every push for social change. We need to take our stories into our own hands."

In her article "A Perspective on Transformative Leadership and African American Women in History," Yvette Lynne Bonaparte writes that African American women have "a rich history of occupying roles as transformative leaders. The tenets of this leadership style have been embraced and effectively leveraged to further social justice." Tyah-Amoy Roberts is in the company of the many Black female transformational leaders who came before her. She is the embodiment of Black women like Fannie Lou Townsend Hamer.

Hamer was one of the most powerful voices and activists of the Black freedom and civil rights movements. She grew up in poverty, picking cotton alongside her parents, who were sharecroppers. The family worked constantly, suffering greatly and receiving no reward for their labor. Living in Mississippi, Hamer was both the subject of and a witness to the violence of racism and discrimination. After attending a Student Nonviolence Coordinating Committee meeting, Hamer volunteered to go to the local courthouse to register to vote, which was illegal for Black people. This was a life-changing moment for Hamer, who felt empowered to confront injustice unapologetically for the first time in her adult life.

As Hamer continued in her activism, she faced violence and threats to her life, but she endured. The confidence and boldness in her voice grew, as did her reputation. She founded the Mississippi Freedom Democratic Party in 1964 and challenged voter suppression. That year she also ran for Congress. At the Democratic National Convention, she delivered the speech that earned her prominence. "If I'm elected as congresswoman, things will be different," Hamer proclaimed. "We are sick and tired of being sick and tired. For so many years, the Negroes have suffered in the state of Mississippi. We are tired of people saying we are satisfied, because we are anything but satisfied."

Hamer's words were powerful and pivotal, and her speech shed light on the struggles Black men and women faced in the pursuit of voting and citizenship rights. She used her oratorical gift and fearlessness to push her agenda of voting rights for Black people and to call out injustice and oppression. She packaged a bold message in each speech: that every individual holds a personal stake in working toward a more just and equitable society.

In an undergraduate thesis titled "Tell It On the Mountain: Fannie Lou Hamer's Pastoral and Prophetic Styles of Leadership as Acts of Public Prayer," University of Montana student Breanna K. Barber writes, "Hamer was blunt in her orations, often criticizing those who did not fight for their right to vote or tried to keep white power structures in place by keeping the African-American community complacent." In a 1965 interview with *Freedomways Magazine*, Hamer said, "There is so much hypocrisy in America. This thing they say of 'the land of the free and the home of the brave' is all on paper. It doesn't mean anything to us. The only way we can make this thing a reality in America is to do all we can to destroy this system and bring this thing out to the light that has been under the cover all these years."

Tyah-Amoy Roberts, who is blunt in her own orations, is similarly critical of any structures that claim to be on the side of liberation while excluding young Black people in America. It has been suggested that young activists like Tyah are following in the footsteps of Martin Luther King Jr. I would argue that Tyah is following in the footsteps of the many women who came before her, such as Fannie Lou Townsend Hamer. Like Hamer, Tyah declares that we exist too; we have a voice too.

Tyah's Leadership Wisdom

Tyah, like the other young Black women in the pages of this book, has figured out how to lead. Below are some of the lessons we can learn from her transformational leadership.

Be Your Most Authentic Self

Tyah believes that the opportunities she has been afforded have happened because of her diligence and commitment to stand for what is right and just. "If I focus on being my most authentic self, then stuff will happen," she says.

Though not a literal formula for success, authenticity is an essential part of honorable living. In a society that encourages us to create idealized images of ourselves in order to fit in, being our truest, most authentic selves is a form of resistance. People hesitate to live as their most authentic selves for many reasons: a fear of vulnerability, a coping strategy for emotional pain, or maybe a natural inclination to seek validation and popularity. But Tyah refuses to put on a false self. With her, who you see is who you get.

Though she exudes this natural confidence in her authenticity, I suspect it is a perpetual challenge for her. For young Black leaders like Tyah, authentic living can be difficult, given the way Black women and girls are marginalized. For most of our lives, we have to evade derogatory and racist stereotypes. Dominant paradigms give us few choices: the Sapphire caricature portrays Black girls as angry, loud, and rude; the Jezebel image portrays Black girls as hypersexualized; and the Mammy image portrays Black women as asexual, devoted caregivers. It can be difficult for Black girls to overcome these labels, doubly marginalized as they are by both race and gender. How can we expect Black girls to live authentically when their personhood is continually vilified?

As a Black teenager, I did not feel the confidence that Tyah presents. I struggled every day to live authentically. I felt constantly pressured to be something or someone other than who I was. I did not feel like I, alone, was enough. As a result, I sometimes gave in to any idea or image I felt would give me social validation, even if it meant being someone other than myself. If I had to change the way I spoke, straighten my hair, tighten my clothes, or even shift my personal values, then I would find a way to conform. This was a false way of living, and one I eventually had to outgrow. Once I challenged myself to discover who I really was, apart from what all those people and spaces pressured me to be, I felt free to live honestly and grew more confident in being my true self in the world.

In his book *The Gift of Being Yourself*, David G. Benner writes, "The self that God persistently loves is not my prettied-up pretend self but my actual self—the real me. But master of delusion that I am, I have trouble penetrating my web of self-deceptions and knowing this real me. I continually confuse it with some ideal self that I wish I were."

The self that Tyah presents to the world is her most authentic self. As she has evolved into a young woman, she has reconciled the person she was created to be with the world around her. Though she knows she is not perfect, she has realized that she, alone, is more than enough.

Be the Example

"I would say that my greatest success as a leader has been inspiring Black girls to do literally whatever they want in life," Tyah explains to me. She pulls herself up from slouching on her couch. Talking about inspiring Black girls clearly invigorates her, and she sits up straight. "After I do speeches and things like that, Black girls come up to me and say, 'I want to do speeches now.' I feel like that's just the coolest thing." One girl came up to her after an event and told her that she'd been watching Tyah for the past two years and that Tyah's activism had inspired her to start her own organization and do similar work. Tyah reminds me that others may be watching the example I set forth. The people watching us will remember how we lived our lives.

Our core beliefs and values must be practiced in front of others. Bearing this responsibility in mind, we live not just for ourselves but aware that our actions could influence someone else—for good or bad. I try to live my life with this knowledge, to be keenly aware that people are watching me. The truth of the matter is that some may be watching in admiration, and others may be waiting for me to make mistakes. Regardless, they are watching. And I hope that even those who are watching for negative reasons can learn something from my life. I want to be an example of what it means to live faithfully. This doesn't mean living perfectly, by any means. We are all imperfect people. Faithful living just means trying your best and keeping in mind that there is an audience watching. My imperfections won't cause me to give up or to stop trying to be the best version of myself.

Prioritize Your Mental Health

Tyah doesn't have many regrets in life, but one thing that does make her uneasy as she looks back is the lack of attention she gave to her mental health following the tragedy at her school. Even though she was not in the building when the shooting occurred, she was, of course, traumatized by the event. In the days and weeks that followed, she attended the funerals of several friends. Crippling anxiety—the realization that she could have been one of the victims—was also in the back of her head. Yet she didn't realize she had trauma to process. She did not seek therapy for two years; when I talked to her, she had just started seeing a counselor at Stanford.

"I could have given more to others had I gotten therapy sooner," Tyah reflects now. "I remember after everything happened, there were counselors and everything, and I thought to myself, 'This is useless and stupid. These people are all white and they don't understand me.' I feel like my greatest failure was ignoring that I actually had trauma to process."

Instead of seeking therapy, Tyah brushed off any emotional damage and looked to move forward quickly and focus on the work at hand. Just when I was wondering whether Tyah's earlier decision not to seek help was connected to the "strong Black woman" trope, she spoke the words that were on my mind: "Avoiding that and trying to be this 'strong Black woman' was my greatest failure."

Society does not give Black women and girls permission to be weak. There is a general sentiment that Black women and girls should be able to handle all things, even beyond the strength that any human being could reasonably exhibit. I wrote about this topic in my book *Parable of the Brown Girl*. While I am a strong, independent Black woman, I can also be vulnerable and fragile. Black women have not had permission to be both. We need to be seen for all of who we are. I am proud of the strength in my DNA as a Black woman and warrior, yet I am also grateful for the grace that gives me space to be weak when I need to be.

Tyah did not feel like she had any space to be weak. She had to be a pillar of strength. While I appreciate the transformational leader she has become, I grieve that she was not able to rest in her vulnerability and pain.

I thought about Tyah's regrets in not tending to her earlier trauma because she minimized her pain. Trauma is any experience that is deeply distressing and that overwhelms our ability to cope. Sometimes people minimize and live in denial about the magnitude of their pain, or they compare their situation to others who they think have it worse. Regardless of their reasoning, pain is pain. To heal from our pain, we must face it. For certain trauma, like Tyah's or other deeply emotional experiences, therapy can allow us a space to both confront our emotional pain and find coping strategies. Caring about and prioritizing our mental health is integral to our well-being. Our mental health affects every aspect of our thoughts, behaviors, and emotions. Poet and activist Audre Lorde said, "Caring for myself is not self-indulgence, it is self-preservation, and that is an act of political warfare." In these days, we must make our emotional and mental health a priority. How can we expect to be any good to anyone else if we are not first being good to ourselves?

Marching for Black Lives

A little over five years before the mass shooting at Marjory Stone-man Douglas High School, a gunman walked into Sandy Hook Elementary School in Newtown, Connecticut, and killed twenty-six people. Twenty of the victims were children between six and eight years old. Tyah was eleven or twelve years old. Of the shooting she says, "I remember seeing it on the news, but then I moved on." At the time she was so young that her mother tried to shield her from that kind of news. *Time* magazine found that between the Sandy Hook shooting in 2012 and the Parkland shooting in 2018, there had been sixty-three school shootings. Tyah only recalls a few of them.

Many people thought the tragedy of an elementary school massacre would spark significant change in gun control legislation in the United States. But although many state-level laws have been passed, major attempts at federal legislation have failed. Tyah's generation has had to grow up with active-shooter drills in school, learning the protocol "Run, Hide, Fight." Even so, she never considered that the violence would reach her own school.

"How are you doing emotionally through all of this?" I ask her. I wonder not just about how she coped during the years following the MSD shooting but also how she as a young person has experienced a contentious social and political climate and a worldwide pandemic.

"I think I'm good right now," she responds. "A few weeks ago [spring 2020], it was very, very hard because it was a pandemic happening, Black people dying, protesting, finishing school [for the year], starting my fellowship. There were so many things happening at once and I was like, 'I can't do it.'"

She stopped attending school lectures and paused on doing homework as a result. For someone as meticulous about her studies as Tyah, this was telling. But she was eventually able to work through it and feels able to move forward.

School still brings her immeasurable joy. She is looking forward to getting more involved with organizations on Stanford's campus, like the school's Black Student Union. She is leaning toward political science for her major but admits that she shunned the idea of going into politics for many years. "I have no idea what my career is going to be, but I know that I love to learn and I love to teach and I like to speak," she says. "I don't know where that will take me. I'm probably going to be a lifelong academic, to be honest, as much as that pains me." She laughs.

Few adults have experienced both the level of trauma and the level of leadership that Tyah has. She is apprehensive about turning twenty. She has had to grow up too fast, so maybe she is holding on to what's left of her adolescence. As long as she is a teenager, her age keeps her in the place from which she should have never been taken in the first place.

Regardless, Tyah has her mind on what she perceives as her life's calling. Like all transformational leaders whose focus is on motivating people to reach their individual potential, Tyah wants Black girls to know they can do whatever they want to do and be whoever they want to be.

"What wakes you up in the morning and gets you doing all this work?" I ask her.

"Black girls, 100 percent," she says. "That's the reason I do literally anything, ever. I want Black girls to feel like 'She's doing it, so I can too.'"

3

LOOKING TO THE FUTURE
THE VISION OF
HANNAH LUCAS

Frankly, we just need to get okay with being not okay. We need to
accept our flaws and love ourselves no matter what.
That's what this app is here for.
−Hannah Lucas, developer of the mobile app notOK

❧

One evening, when Hannah Lucas's mother was getting ready
for bed, she stopped at the top of the stairs to check on Hannah. She knew that her fifteen-year-old daughter had been facing
bullying and harassment at school and that Hannah was warding
off depression. Her mother did not know how deep that state of
despair was, however, nor that her daughter believed there was
only one way to escape the unbearable pain.

Hannah's mother happened to open the bedroom door just as
Hannah was putting a handful of pills in her mouth. "I ran over

to her, and I grabbed her, and I fished them out. And she was just like, 'I don't want to be here anymore. I can't take it anymore,'" her mother recalled in an interview.

In the next moment, says Hannah's mother, Hannah screamed out the words that would change the trajectory of her life and vocation: "I just wish there was a button I could press!"

Amid her desperation and anguish, Hannah had a vision.

Thankfully, Hannah would survive that night, and with the help of her mother, she would live to share this experience. Now Hannah channels her energies into helping others who find themselves in a similar state of hopelessness. "No one thought I would ever get better," she says. "It is a miracle that I can drive or even that I graduated from high school." She pauses. "My mom saved my life."

Hannah Lucas is more than a miracle. Hannah Lucas is a survivor with a story to tell.

And her story begins that night when she tried to end her life; it begins in a deep moment of despair and distress, and with a vision for a button someone could press for help.

Withering Away

For most of her childhood, Hannah was a competitive gymnast. While she loved the sport, she felt gymnastics was taking up too much of her schedule, so she quit to free up more of her time. The relief of having a lighter schedule was interrupted when she began to experience symptoms of a chronic illness. It started with severe headaches, and over time, the illness became more tormenting. One day the school nurse called her mother to tell her Hannah had passed out. Eventually she began passing out almost every day, and her mother would have to pick her up from school.

"I was experiencing concussive symptoms," Hannah recalls. "I would have brain fog. I could never focus on what I was doing. I started fainting and passing out, and I had super low blood pressure."

The doctors could not figure out what was wrong with her. Some doctors displayed a level of distrust in Hannah as she reported what she was experiencing. "I was a teenage girl, and doctors didn't really believe my symptoms," she tells me. "I went from doctor to doctor. Some thought I was faking or that I wanted attention. They were like, 'She's just depressed' and put me on antidepressants. Or they thought I was faking to get out of school."

Hannah's experience—as a teenaged Black girl being misdiagnosed by white medical professionals—is one element of an unfortunate larger story. Black women's and girls' health and medical outcomes are frequently endangered by a medical establishment not designed for them. Indeed, the Black Women's Heath Imperative poses a provocative question: "What if all Black women & girls enjoyed optimal health and well-being in a socially just society?"

Discriminatory patterns—lack of access, racialized health disparities, dismissive responses from medical professionals—are deeply troubling. Hannah says it is imperative for the healthcare industry to prioritize Black women's and girls' health. "There are so many medical fails with Black women especially, because, first, we're women. And then on top of that, we're Black, so doctors are prone to thinking we're being overly dramatic. Then we're perceived as being stronger than what we are."

Hannah received several different and conflicting diagnoses. At one point a doctor thought she had lupus and then, after an MRI, thought she had cancer. After a few weeks the results came back negative. This process was not only frustrating but scary for Hannah.

Eventually Hannah was diagnosed with Postural Orthostatic Tachycardia Syndrome, or POTS, a disorder of the autonomic nervous system that affects blood circulation. "I was strong, and then all of a sudden I needed basic help like walking," she recalls. She was put on medication, was told to maintain good exercise and hydration, and was consistently monitored.

As a result of her illness, specifically her frequent passing out and seizures, Hannah became a victim of extreme bullying, harassment, and threats in high school. Along with talking about Hannah behind her back, some students would fake seizures to mock her. "I would hear people talking about me and I would be standing right behind them [and they were] saying, 'Yeah, this girl is so weird—she has seizures.'" She'd hear other horrible comments too, like, "It would be my lucky day if I found her passed out." Hannah attributes the bullying to the fact that she was a good student—as well as the only Black girl in her classes. In addition to making fun of her illness, white students made fun of her hair and used the N-word around her.

Even though Hannah had been an honors student, she began having a difficult time making it through her classes. Her illness made it hard for her to concentrate, and between that and the bullying, she struggled. By the end of her first year of high school, she had missed 196 classes due to her condition.

Hannah tried to persevere. "This goes back to being raised in a predominantly white area because not only am I a girl, but I am a Black girl," she reflects now. "A saying in my house was that you have to try twice as hard in order to be seen as half as good compared to everyone else. So many Black girls hear that, and so many are raised with that idea. Because of the truth of it, we put so much unneeded pressure on ourselves."

Hannah's depression got worse, which led to a struggle with disordered eating. She would go days without eating and then binge-eat until she vomited. From there, she began to engage in self-harm.

Hannah explains her reasoning from that era to me now: "Depression isn't when you feel all of the sadness in the world. It is when you stop feeling." Hannah pauses. It's clear that recalling that time of life is not easy for her. "So that's why I started cutting: because I wanted to feel anything, even if it was pain. I remember my dog would want to snuggle or play with me, and I didn't even crack a smile. That's when it started to freak me out."

Things got progressively worse. Hannah began to bleach her skin to try to make it lighter. As she describes these types of self-harm, I realize that her experience isn't an isolated one. One of the girls I interviewed for *Parable of the Brown Girl*, Leah, struggled with depression and found unhealthy ways of coping with her insecurities. "I self-harmed because I wanted to see my pain on me," Leah once admitted to me.

Like Hannah, Leah also struggled with an eating disorder: "I felt out of control based on the fact that I have darker skin and kinkier hair. Every time I looked in the mirror, I felt broken, and I couldn't control those aspects of myself, so I became obsessed with controlling my weight."

The crisis of Black youth suicide attempts is alarming. A 2019 article in *US News and World Report* indicated that "suicide attempts increased at an accelerating rate among black female teens." While it can be difficult to ascertain the direct reason for these rates, the crisis is going largely unnoticed.

In Hannah's case, her mother was fully aware that Hannah was struggling; she just didn't know the depths to which that emotional struggle went. "I witnessed her completely just wither away every single day. Her light just dimmed," Hannah's mother recalled. Seeing her mother's concern grieved Hannah. She felt guilty about the trouble her illness, the bullying, and the resulting depression caused her loved ones. Not only did she carry her own pain, but she felt she was the source of her mother's pain too. Hannah was experiencing a silent crisis, and her pain was reaching its tipping point.

notOK App

After years of battling depression, Hannah decided that the only way to ease the pain was to die by suicide. "That night, my mom saved my life during my suicide attempt. When she was holding me, I just remember my thumb." Hannah motions with her thumb now, to show me what she did that night. After her mother got the pills out of her mouth and as she held her tight, Hannah made a motion with her thumb, as though she were pressing down on something. Hannah saw a vision of herself pressing an app on her phone.

Hannah intuited something in that moment. She realized that others who are in emotional, mental, or physical distress may not be as fortunate as she was to have someone right there to help save them. Instead, in that moment, they would reach for what they had there with them: their phones. According to one survey, Americans check their phones ninety-six times a day. Other survey data suggests that 51 percent of people check apps on their phone one to ten times per day. What Hannah imagined was a digital panic button of sorts—a method by which someone in need of help could call out to a loved one.

"I just wanted something that I could physically press that wasn't a life alarm necklace," she says. "I just remember wanting an app on my phone that I could press."

A little over a week after the incident, as she regained emotional strength and reflected on her distress that evening, Hannah could not get the idea of the app out of her head. She realized that, if she were to ever be in that position again, she wanted certain people to know she was not okay, and she wanted them to know where to find her. For Hannah, an app would be something she could use for both her mental illness and her chronic illness. She knew this vision was intended to benefit not only herself but others who find themselves in a similar position of need.

Hannah began to research whether an app like she envisioned already existed—one she just hadn't heard of. But nothing of this kind existed. "I told my brother about it," says Hannah, "and he goes, 'I got you. Let's go. I can make this.' And so he did."

When Hannah's brother, Charlie, was seven years old, he had taught himself how to build apps and programs, so he already had the basic skills necessary. For his sister's app idea, he first made the wireframe, which is the workflow and plan for how the app would look and function. He then made the basic prototype of the app. From there, the siblings eventually found developers to help with creating the app. While Charlie worked on the technical part, Hannah worked on the business side, researching how to form a limited liability company and thinking through how to best market the app. In the midst of it all, Hannah also entered intensive therapy and life coaching to help with her mental health.

Hannah and Charlie knew they had to get two important stakeholders—their parents—on board with the idea. So the two of them also created a fifteen-page presentation about the app to show to their parents to prove to them that they were serious about the project. Proud and impressed, their parents promised to support their new venture.

Hannah and Charlie named the app notOK—because, as their slogan says, "It's okay to be notOK." When it launched, the notOK app became exactly the resource Hannah had envisioned: a digital panic button that, when pressed, sends an alert for help. The notOK app can send that alert to up to five preselected contacts to let them know that the person is not okay. It also automatically sends out the distressed person's GPS location and directions to get there.

What began as a vision and an idea is now an app with more than 70,000 users who have hit the notOK button at least 50,000 times.

The website for notOK (www.notOKapp.com) lists Hannah, Charlie, and their dog, Trooper (whose responsibilities are "emotional support and encouragement"), as part of the notOK team. The website also lists important facts about mental health, such as that one in four people worldwide struggles mentally or emotionally. It mentions that suicide is the second leading cause of death in youth ages thirteen to twenty-four. The website also includes information about support groups and resources for people struggling with mental health issues, alongside the option to download other apps. Since the launch of the app, Hannah has emerged as a spokesperson for Black women's mental health. She and Charlie have been invited to speak and be interviewed for numerous events and organizations.

Hannah attributes part of the appeal of the app to the fact that it takes the guesswork out of asking for help. There remains a stigma around asking for help. According to Hannah, our society should normalize seeking help.

"Sometimes I forget that people are actually using the app!" Hannah tells me. She has a humble and friendly spirit, and she laughs just as much with her big brown eyes as she does with her smile. "Sometimes I'll go to the app store and look at the reviews. One has really stuck with me. It was from a parent saying, 'Thank you for creating this app and I definitely recommend it for anyone that's struggling. My daughter pressed the notOK button instead of jumping out of her bedroom window.'"

Other users have written similar testimonials: "This app alerted my mom that I was not ok and she showed up very fast," one user wrote. "Sometimes when I'm having a panic attack, I can't sit and text—from shaking or I just can't think clearly. This app makes it easy to let people know you're NOT ok and you need help," another said. One user simply wrote: "Such a great app to save lives!"

Hannah and her brother Charlie—and their dog, Trooper—are doing just that.

Visionary Leadership

In their article "Visionary Leadership and Strategic Management," Frances Westley and Henry Mintzberg, professors of management at McGill University in Montreal, write that visionary leadership usually tracks a three-step process, beginning with a vision (idea), moving to communication (word), and finally empowerment (action). In Hannah's case, she first had her vision. Next, she communicated it to her brother, who responded eagerly with the words "Let's go!" Westley and Mintzberg write, "What distinguishes visionary leadership is that through words and actions, the leader gets the followers to 'see' his or her vision—to see a new way to think and act—and so to join their leader in realizing it." Charlie was inspired by

Hannah's vision and got on board with helping her actualize it. This led to the last part of the process, in which the two of them worked to bring that vision into action.

Hannah was determined to turn her vision into a reality. Her visionary leadership through the development of the notOK app has saved lives by transforming the difficult task of asking for help into an action as simple as pressing a button. A visionary leader has a gift for making their idea a reality. They hold a vision for the future and simultaneously inspire others to help make it come to pass. As Randy Grieser, CEO of Achieve Centre for Leadership and Work Performance, writes, "Vision is our view of the future. Vision is the portrait of our hopes and dreams. It is our mental picture of what might be, but is not yet."

A visionary is an imaginative person who has the ability to think ahead and plan out the future in an efficient and intelligent way. When I asked Hannah to describe herself, she said "imaginative and creative." Hannah's visionary leadership is bold and innovative, yet she also displays a service-oriented style that keeps her grounded and centered. "Being a leader is having an idea and acting on the idea for the benefit of the masses instead of the minority," Hannah says. Hannah always has the people she intends to serve in mind to encourage her to keep going. She fixates on ensuring that anyone who is struggling like she was that night will have the help they need.

Amid one of her most difficult and life-altering moments, Hannah had a vision. While she saw herself pressing a button that would save her life, she was also manifesting a future reality. She was envisioning other people in a similar position who would one day use that button—which didn't yet exist—to save their own lives. What Hannah saw had yet to come to fruition, but it was there in her future. She just needed to create a plan to get there.

Creator Visionary

Along with the process of visionary leadership, Westley and Mintzberg describe distinct styles of visionary leaders. In their rubric, Hannah's style makes her a "creator visionary." Creator visionaries are characterized by the originality of their inventions, in addition to the practical and holistic quality of a vision's realization. Creator visionaries are typically entrepreneurial by nature. They frequently create startups, like Hannah did with notOK. Creator visionaries focus on creating products that are tangible and accessible to consumers. The notOK app is about making the process as easy and simple as possible for its users to get the help they need. Finally, Westley and Mintzberg write—and they may as well be describing Hannah—"Vision for the creator occurs in moments of inspiration, which seize the leader suddenly and unexpectedly and which become, for that leader, a driving preoccupation, the single-minded focus which evokes, at least metaphorically, the notion of all eyes turned in a single direction." Hannah's moment of despair became a moment of inspiration. She saw a vision of herself pressing a button. In that moment she was seized suddenly and unexpectedly with a vision for what would become the notOK app, which is now her life's mission.

Westley and Mintzberg suggest that "vision is often experienced as deriving from a source outside the self, as in the classic case of religious leaders who claim to be the receptacles or channels of divine inspiration." While Hannah does not claim to have had any religious type of vision in that moment, she says she has indeed leaned on her faith in difficult times. "Faith is what keeps people going," she says—faith that is, as the writer of Hebrews says, "the substance of things hoped for, the evidence of things not seen" (Hebrews 13:1 KJV).

Harriet Tubman's Divine Visions

The idea of divinely inspired foresight—that people are sometimes given visions of a future that has yet to unfold, along with direction for how to be part of that future—has long and deep roots in Black religious traditions. Harriet Tubman, known as the Moses of her people for helping more than seventy enslaved individuals make their way to freedom, said she had always had the spiritual gift of protective foresight, which she believed was generationally inherited. However, it was after a violent encounter that her visions became more vivid.

At the age of twelve, Harriet Tubman encountered an enraged overseer, who threw a heavy metal weight that hit her in the head and severely injured her. Tubman suffered from the debilitating results of this violent event for the rest of her life: headaches, fainting spells, epileptic seizures, and even narcolepsy, causing her to go into sleep-like states during the day. She also had vivid dreams and saw visions that she was convinced were communications from God.

In an interview, Tubman's great-great-great-grandniece Ernestine Martin Wyatt confirmed her understanding of the occurrences and of Tubman's foresight, saying, "She did have visions . . . she asked God to use her as a vessel and the visions came to her, during those seizures." Through these visions, Tubman felt God was guiding and directing her. She sometimes knew about things that would happen before they occurred. Based on her research, Kasi Lemmons, co-writer of the film *Harriet*, says

Tubman even claimed she saw the end of slavery several years before the Emancipation Proclamation. "She woke up from the vision and said to her abolitionist friend, 'My people are free!'" Lemmons recounts. "And her friend said, 'My dear, not in our lifetime.' And Harriet said, 'No, God just showed me. My people are free.' When the Emancipation Proclamation happened and people were celebrating, her friend said to her, 'Why aren't you celebrating?' [Tubman] said, 'I celebrated two years ago.'"

In addition to seeing the end of slavery, Harriet Tubman had premonitions about her role in freeing slaves. Tubman's righteous vision played a significant role in leading her to rescue and free enslaved people through the Underground Railroad. Hannah Lucas's and Harriet Tubman's stories are clearly different. Yet they share similarities in terms of vision birthed through difficult circumstances. Their visions were not only of a better life for themselves; they were visions that would liberate others along their journey.

Hannah's Leadership Wisdom

Hannah has learned a lot about leadership and healing and about what true strength means—lessons many of us take years of adulthood to grasp.

It's Okay to Not Be Okay

The entire premise of the notOK app is that "it is okay to not be okay." This is both the motto of the business and the message Hannah intends to communicate to the world. As she shared her vision for notOK by telling me her life story, I reflected on times when I purported to be okay while I was, in fact, not okay. As a young person and even into adulthood, I always felt like I had to have it all together. As a Black woman, I have always felt like I must be strong.

Some years ago, I went through a difficult emotional season, but every time friends would ask how I was doing, I would smile and say, "I'm good!" The concerned looks on their faces gave away the fact that they didn't believe me, and many of them would ask me again. I would stand my ground about how well I was doing and proceed to list all the projects I was working on to demonstrate my (false) superhuman strength. But I wasn't good. I was not okay. Unfortunately, it took years for me to lean into the discomfort of not being okay, to let my loved ones know, and to ask for help. I was an adult when I began that process, and even now, I must continue to remind myself that it is okay to be disappointed. It is okay to be hurt. It is okay to not have things figured out. It is okay to feel lost. We must accept that it is okay to not be okay and to feel whatever we feel in life's unyielding moments.

It's Okay to Be Unique

Hannah has risen above the worst of what has been said and done to her with a message that it is okay to be uncommon, and it is okay to be unique. "I want people to see my story and see everything I did to alter the way I look," Hannah explains. "I tried to straighten my hair. I tried skin bleaching. I altered the way that I talked. I put on my white girl voice. I'm sure every single Black person has that. I just tried fitting in so badly, but I was always different, and I just want people to know that it's okay to be different."

Every single individual has something unique about them, whether in their physicality or their personality. In *The Purpose Driven Life*, pastor Rick Warren writes, "God prescribed every single detail of your body. He deliberately chose your race, the color of your skin, your hair, and every other feature. He custom-made your body just the way he wanted it. He also determined the natural talents you would possess and the uniqueness of your personality. The Bible says [Psalm 139:15 MSG], 'You know me inside and out, you know every bone in my body; You know exactly how I was made, bit by bit, how I was sculpted from nothing into something.'"

God designed our unique makeup, with intention. God gave us all the permission we need to be ourselves. Unfortunately, society does not give all of us that same approval. From Hannah I learn that our uniqueness should not be hidden away. Our individuality is one of the greatest assets we can offer this world. You are the only one of you in the world, and that is okay.

It's Okay to Love Yourself

Self-love may sound simple enough as a concept, but it proves difficult for many people because it requires ignoring or removing the harmful stigmas of outside influences. Outside voices and opinions often have tremendous effect on our self-worth. Yet our own opinion of ourselves is what matters most.

"Everything with the app, and my therapy and life coaching, has forced me to take a look at myself and forced me to love every single aspect of myself," Hannah says. "This is difficult in a society that targets you every single chance they get."

What does it mean to love ourselves? Author, professor, and social activist bell hooks has written that self-love means seeing and accepting ourselves as we truly are. In her book *All About Love: New Visions*, she shared a powerful thought about how to envision self-love: "One of the best guides to how to be self-loving is to give ourselves the love we are often dreaming about receiving from others. There was a time when I felt lousy about my over-forty body, saw myself as too fat, too this, or too that. Yet I fantasized about finding a lover who would give me the gift of being loved as I am. It is silly, isn't it, that I would dream of someone else offering to me the acceptance and affirmation I was withholding from myself."

What pertinent advice: to "give ourselves the love we are often dreaming about receiving from others." If I apply bell hooks's wisdom, then I envision giving myself more understanding. I envision giving myself more grace. I, like hooks, envision the gift of being loved as I am. Hannah has made this journey to self-love a personal practice; it's another important part of her "it's okay" message of hope to others.

"Learn how to love every single aspect of you," Hannah advises. "Learn how to love the very essence of yourself, and then it'll make whatever you do in life that much easier because you won't care about how people perceive you."

Looking to the Future

Hannah was recently featured as one of *Teen Vogue*'s "21 Under 21." The December 2020 article was titled "The Girls and Femmes Building a Better Future." In the same month, she took part in an episode of Jada Pinkett Smith's *Red Table Talk* that featured the testimonials of people who have survived suicide attempts and are now helping others find meaning and purpose in life. These are just two of the many ways Hannah has been able to share her story and become a source of hope for others.

Still, she is an everyday eighteen-year-old girl who loves to spend time with her friends. Hannah currently attends Georgia State University, taking online classes due to the COVID-19 pandemic. She wants to major in social entrepreneurship, because one day she hopes to be "the Amazon of the fashion industry." While fashion is her creative passion, mental health is what she calls her "social passion."

"Fashion is something I have always loved, but mental health just kind of snuck up on me when I was struggling, and I realized how important it is," she says. "People don't really realize it's that important, so I need to fight for it."

Hannah was a part of the graduating class of 2020, whose senior year was disrupted due to the pandemic. She missed out on typical experiences like prom and graduation. "I was going to be prom queen," she tells me. "Then COVID-19 decided to strike." In May of that year, Hannah created a virtual prom for students who were members of the class of 2020, many of whom were devastated by the abrupt ending of their school year and disappointed by the loss of monumental occasions like prom. She named it "We Are All Well: Prom 2020." Hannah and her brother Charlie hosted the virtual prom, which featured celebrities including DJ Jazzy Jeff. The class of 2020 holds a special place in Hannah's heart, not just because she was a part of it, but because she is proud to be a member of this resilient generation.

"I love my generation so much," she tells me. "I could go on and on about how legendary my generation is. 'Legendary' is the only way to describe us. We're funny but we're also vulnerable, and we find strength in our vulnerability. Not only that, but we stand for justice and we're willing to learn. Being willing to learn is what sets my generation apart from so many others."

In describing her generation, Hannah certainly describes herself. Hannah is an inspiration to those of us who have experienced low moments in life. She demonstrates that there is hope on the other side of anguish. Furthermore, Hannah recognizes the responsibility that comes with the attention her leadership has gotten. She takes her role as a leader and guide very seriously.

"I don't want anyone feeling the way I did," she says. "Especially other little Black girls. I want them to be able to find people who they can look up to who look like them. Black girls come in all different shades, personalities, and life experiences. I want them to see a range of their emotions."

Since the launch of the notOK app, Hannah has been busy putting more of her vision for healing and hope into action. "We're actually doing a big update soon that's going to go global. We're going to expand into Canada and the UK, and it's going to tie into the crisis text line." She is also in the early stages of creating a consulting company. It will be centered on Black teenagers because she thinks a lot of people follow the trends that Black teenagers set.

"I am the type of person that when I put my mind to something, it's going to happen," she says. This is certainly demonstrated in her creation of the app. By pursuing that vision of herself pressing a button, she has transformed her own pain and suffering into a future in which others are freer.

HAPPINESS AS HOPE
THE SERVANT LEADERSHIP OF GRACE CALLWOOD

I am a strong believer that there is no age limit on service.
–Grace Callwood, founder and chairwoman of
The We Cancerve Movement, Inc.

✦

W hen Grace Callwood was almost seven years old, her grand-mother noticed a lump on Grace's neck. Grace's mother, T'Jae Ellis, immediately scheduled an appointment with the pedia-trician. The appointment fell on Grace's birthday. T'Jae directly asked the doctor if she should be worried about lymphoma, since the swelling was near Grace's lymph nodes. She doesn't know what motivated her to ask that, but she recalls a clear prompting—some maternal instinct that told her something was wrong.

Listening to T'Jae tell the story years later, I notice she is visibly troubled as she remembers the flippant response of the doctor. "She thought I had braided her hair too tight, and that it was causing an inflamed scalp. And I'm thinking, 'No, this is crazy!'" T'Jae exclaims. "She made a horrible assumption, which I'm now starting to understand as some of the racial implications of pediatric medicine."

T'Jae tried to tell the doctor that she couldn't be braiding Grace's hair too tightly, because her hair was so soft. But the pediatrician went ahead and prescribed a cream for the swelling—a medication that insurance didn't cover. That night, on the drive to the pharmacy, T'Jae cried the entire time. She wondered if she was just being paranoid, an overly concerned mother whose mind was going to the worst-case scenario. Yet she couldn't dismiss what she felt in her gut: the doctor was missing something essential.

One week later, T'Jae noticed another lump, this time on Grace's thigh. Again, Grace's grandmother encouraged them to go to the doctor—a different one—immediately. But T'Jae and Grace felt uncomfortable in that practice as well, sensing that the doctor was rushing through the appointment and not listening to them. That was October 5, 2011.

T'Jae went home, did more research, and managed to get an appointment for Grace with yet another doctor for the next day. This time, the response was different. "The chief of pediatric surgery took one look at her and said that she needed to go into surgery," T'Jae says.

On October 7, Grace went into surgery to have a lymph node in her neck removed. On October 9, she was diagnosed with cancer. The doctors could not pinpoint the type of cancer at first; it was either non-Hodgkins lymphoma or leukemia. That night

T'Jae and Grace went home to pack, preparing to move into the hospital, where Grace would stay for the next ten to thirteen days.

"To us it seemed like an eternity," T'Jae recalls. Grace had just started the first grade.

It had been two and a half weeks since they first noticed the lump. T'Jae believed that had it not been for her mother's persistence in encouraging them to see another doctor, they would not have gotten a diagnosis that quickly. Her mother had noticed how annoyed T'Jae was after the first pediatrician prescribed the skin cream, having assumed the lump was caused by tight hair-braiding. What if T'Jae hadn't been so determined about getting a second and then a third opinion? What if she hadn't been skeptical about the doctor's theory and hadn't advocated for her daughter? "I wrestled with this for years," Grace's mother reflects now.

After completing extensive chemotherapy and other types of treatment, Grace went into remission. After five years, they found no trace of cancer in her system and Grace was declared cured. Yet the pain and sense of being failed by the medical establishment remains. "The timing is right for us to have this part of that conversation, with what is going on in this country and in this world," T'Jae says. "We're looking at these microaggressions and so-called subtleties of racism. And I never really thought about it until recently, and I'm thinking, 'What is up with that?' The first pediatrician missed the call."

Grace was the victim of a subconscious stereotype and of a doctor's knowledge gap that led to misinformation and a misdiagnosis. We now know the ways implicit bias affects Black women's experiences in the healthcare system. Writing about the racial disparities that affect Black women's health, Dr. Nataki Douglas says, "Further complicating matters is the reality of implicit bias—meaning the attitudes and stereotypes in our subconscious that affect how we view and treat people—and how that impacts the care that Black women receive."

"This is real talk for real women," says T'Jae. "Especially women of color. How many instances do we find ourselves in where we are made to second-guess ourselves and made to feel inadequate or overreacting for things that are legitimately given audience for any other group of people?"

The We Cancerve Movement

"Callwood. That's C-a-l-l-w-o-o-d," Grace says at the beginning of our conversation, making sure I get the spelling of her last name correct. When we chat, she is fifteen years old and going into the tenth grade. Grace has long flowing braids and is wearing a yellow T-shirt that brings out the glow of her beautiful chocolate complexion. She refers to herself as the "happiness fairy," and it's clearly an apt description.

Grace considers herself much like any other teenage girl. She loves binge-watching Netflix shows with her mother—"I watched *Glee* all the way through—twice," she laughs—and she has a passionate love for music. "I love Amy Winehouse," she says, and then lists out other artists she enjoys: Carole King, the Beatles, and crooners like Frank Sinatra and Tony Bennett. She is certainly what some people call "an old soul."

"I'm in the marching band at my high school," she says, and lists her personal commitments and hobbies outside of school. "I play the French horn. I am in the liturgical dance group at my church. I'm also in the youth choir at my church and, of course, community service." Service is a given for Grace. It is not only what she does; it is who she is.

Not long after Grace was diagnosed with cancer—which turned out to be non-Hodgkins lymphoma—a friend told her about a family who had just lost their home in a fire. That family had two little girls. "All I could think of was that I had just entered sickness and they had just entered homelessness," Grace remembers.

She decided to give the girls her brand-new back-to-school clothes. The medicine Grace was taking made her gain and lose weight constantly, and she soon felt she didn't have a need for most of her clothes anymore. Grace's mom made the delivery, and when Grace heard about how happy the girls were, she knew she wanted to do more. With the help of her mother and grandmother, a still-sick Grace narrowed down a broad list to the specific groups she wanted to serve.

While undergoing cancer treatment, Grace was a Wish Kid through the Make-a-Wish Foundation, an organization that creates life-changing wishes for children with critical illnesses. For her wish, she traveled to Disney World, where a "gift fairy" distributed gifts to her and the other children. Having decided she didn't need the toys, Grace donated them to a local homeless shelter.

During this time, Grace was enduring the agony of constant treatment. "Physically and emotionally, I was drained," she says. Grace underwent chemotherapy for three and a half years. For the first nine months after her initial diagnosis, she had a spinal tap procedure every week. On average Grace took ten medications per day, and at one point she was taking thirty-five pills every single day. At times it was too difficult for her to balance her ambition and passion to serve others with her illness, but Grace persevered.

"A bit after that, I had gained some more strength back," Grace recounts. "I did a lemonade stand in my driveway on a Saturday in the summer. We sold lemonade for a dollar a cup, and we wound up raising $633. That kind of showed me, my mom, and the community that I was truly able to make a difference and that people believed in me."

One year after her diagnosis, when Grace was only eight, she started an organization to "bring happiness to some of society's most vulnerable youth: children experiencing home-lessness, illness, and who are in foster care." The name, The We Cancerve Movement, is a clever wordplay that transforms the bleakness of the word *cancer* by fusing it with the hopeful-ness of service.

Though T'Jae realized that serving others was important to Grace, she wanted their focus to remain on Grace's health. She loved Grace's invigorating passion for service, but she did not want it to come at the expense of her healing. As Grace contin-ued her treatment, she also kept working on different projects to show her mother she was serious about starting an organization. Eventually they decided to move forward with it and came up with the name and logo.

From there, Grace created a youth-led board of advisors, who are all between the ages of eight and eighteen. In its first year, the organi-zation had thirteen board members. Grace lights up when she speaks of her organization and its foundations. What is often traumatic for cancer survivors to think back on—the period when they were the most ill and their future most uncertain—Grace remembers as the challenging yet hopeful birth of a burgeoning movement.

"I have definitely grown a lot and learned a ton. Starting off, it was just a lot of realizing that I could really make a difference," she says.

The We Cancerve Movement's vision is "to change the way adults think about youth leadership in philanthropic and business communities by influencing a generation of social changemakers determined to provide solutions that bring vulnerable children happiness . . . swiftly!"

The We Cancerve Movement currently has a total of twenty initiatives, including the following:

- Books & Buddies, which donates books to help young children pass the hours of infusions during their chemo treatments

- Breakfast Bags Bonanza, which rallies community support to help provide individual servings of breakfast food items distributed to children at area homeless shelters and transitional housing programs, foster care group homes and orphanages, local community feeding programs, and Title I schools

- Gift to Give, which helps children living at homeless shelters and transitional housing programs give their parents or guardians a gift for Christmas

- We Cancerve Children's Libraries, which provide free books to foster, at-risk, and hospitalized children

- Camp Happy, a free summer enrichment day camp for youth who are homeless or in foster care and includes field trips to local places like dairy farms, movie theaters, swimming pools, and equestrian centers

To date, the organization and its volunteers have helped more than 23,000 children and families, all because Grace channeled what was a life-threatening obstacle into a life-changing enterprise.

The Servant Leader

In a 2009 interview with human rights activist and theologian Desmond Tutu, the interviewer asks him, "What in your opinion makes a good leader?" Tutu responds, "Ultimately you want a leader who is also a servant." Mentioning Nelson Mandela, Gandhi, Martin Luther King Jr., and Mother Teresa, Tutu notes that their leadership was sacrificial: designed for the sake of those they were serving. Tutu reminds us that servant leaders do not lead for self-glorification. Grace is the personification of a servant leader.

Servant leadership, a term coined by Robert Greenleaf, the founder of the Greenleaf Center for Applied Ethics, is an intuitive approach to life. Greenleaf writes, "The servant-leader is servant first. . . . It begins with the natural feeling that one wants to serve, to serve first." This would explain why leadership appears to come so effortlessly to Grace. Her leadership grows out of a deeply held desire to serve others.

Servant-leaders are "closer to the ground," writes Greenleaf: "they hear things, see things, know things, and their intuitive insight is exceptional." This intuitive insight is in evidence as Grace reflects on the time just following her diagnosis, when she says she blamed herself for her illness. "As a seven-year-old, you think if something bad happens, it might be because you did something bad. So I figured, 'What did I do wrong to make cancer happen to me?' I want to make sure other kids in sad situations know that it's not their fault and that another kid was thinking about them and considering them." As she heals from her own illness, she seeks to heal others.

Based on Greenleaf's definition, then, Larry Spears identified unique characteristics of servant leaders. While Grace's leadership reflects many of these, three in particular stand out:

- The ability to actively listen to others
- Empathy toward others
- Commitment to promoting healing of others in need

As a leader, Grace knows how to strike a balance between serving others and preserving one's own sense of self. "One of my greatest successes as a leader is being able to stay true to who I am, and having a spirit of learning and also being aware of the needs of others," Grace says. As a servant leader, Grace listens intently to the needs of the youth she serves, her board of directors, and the community around her. It is very important to her to give people what they need and what they ask for. She believes that some organizations mistakenly *assume* what their constituency needs and give services based on those assumptions. Instead, Grace seeks to address the needs directly. She is also attentive about the needs of her board. Realizing that her board members may not always grasp how much work is involved, she takes time to care for and guide her team. She wants her board members to be happy and comfortable and to have the resources they need to lead a successful organization.

Black Women's Servant Leadership

Grace stands in a long line of Black women who are servant leaders. While Black men typically took public roles during the civil rights movement, Black women's leadership occupied a central position in the movement. "Servant leadership has been in practice by African American women and even women who may not have been considered as leaders," writes Debora Y. Marina in their article "Servant Leaders Who Picked Up the Broken Glass." Working behind the scenes, Black women often received less attention, with their leadership lacking the exposure the men's activism garnered.

But we can celebrate their work now.

Dorothy Height organized the 1963 March on Washington. Xernona Clayton Brady investigated acts of racial injustice against Black employees and organized events for the Southern Christian Leadership Conference. Septima Poinsette Clark was an advocate for education who became known as the "mother of the civil rights movement." Daisy Bates championed the integration of public schools and served as a mentor to the Little Rock Nine, the first Black students to attend Central High School in Little Rock, Arkansas. "These women didn't stand on ceremony; they simply did the work that needed to be done, without expectation of personal gain," writes Janet Dewart Bell in *The Nation*. "Often unnamed or underappreciated, African-American women helped to construct the cultural architecture for change." Bell suggests that Black women's servant leadership was rooted in their desire to serve communities, and that this form of authority was not about gaining power or exercising top-down leadership. This bottom-up approach characterized Black women's work prior to the civil rights movement as well, through many of our foremothers in preceding generations.

One of Grace's main inspirations is servant leader Marian Wright Edelman, the founder and president of the Children's Defense Fund. Edelman devoted her life to helping disadvantaged children, as well as to ending inequality and child poverty. Grace thinks Edelman's philosophy on work and life aligns with hers. "Service is the rent that each of us pays for living," Edelman once said, "the very purpose of life and not something you do in your spare time." Grace's entire worldview stems from a life of service.

Unfortunately—for the women of the civil rights movement, for Grace, and for all of us—the power of Black women's servant leadership has often been perceived as passive and weak. This form of leadership is frequently seen as the backdrop to leadership that stands on the front lines. Servant leadership, however, is not the same as servility. Servant leadership is not a passive, submissive eagerness to benefit others. The servant leader's power and authority lie in their willingness to put others first; they are active and intentional. Their greatness is that they lead, no matter what their position is.

Robert Greenleaf was far from the first to propose servant leadership as a concept. Jesus spoke of the nuances of servant leadership when he said, "Whoever wants to be great among you must be your servant" (Matthew 20:26 NET). Elsewhere he said, "Anyone who wants to be first must be the very last, and the servant of all" (Mark 9:35 NIV). Jesus reframed traditional leadership by placing service first. Here, greatness in leadership is defined by putting the welfare of others above one's own. Servant leadership is not concerned with superior ranking. If it is true that "good leaders must first become good servants," then Black women and girls like Grace have been at the forefront of superior leadership since the dawn of time.

Sojourner Truth, American abolitionist, women's rights activist, and a true servant leader, is often attributed with the quote, "I will not allow my life's light to be determined by the darkness around me." Grace lives her life channeling this same passion and dedication. Like Sojourner Truth, Grace would not allow the darkness of her cancer diagnosis to keep her from being a light to those in need around her.

Grace's Leadership Wisdom

In her short life, Grace has demonstrated numerous dimensions of leadership that we can learn from.

Joy Is an Act of Resistance

Grace recalls a time when she was at the hospital during one of her rounds of surgery and treatments. She doesn't remember much because to her it all went by so quickly, but what she does recall is feeling happy just to be there with her mother, playing card games.

"Moving into the hospital, I was okay with missing school," she reflects. "My mom and I got to play Uno more. It was just something different." She did miss playing with her friends and was in a measure of physical pain. Yet in the moment, Grace picked out that one thing that brought her joy and held on to it.

"I just kind of went with it, because I didn't know what to think or do," Grace recalls. "Being a sick kid, I had no idea what cancer was or what it did until I had it, so the entire journey was a learning process for me. . . . I just remember going to the doctor a lot. Them saying I had cancer didn't do anything for me. . . . I didn't know what that meant for me or my life. I just knew I had to get through it."

Grace radiates an inherent joy. When I first began to research, read about, and watch videos of Grace, I couldn't stop smiling; a "happiness fairy" indeed! I have heard the phrase "Joy is an act of resistance" many times, but I have seen the phrase manifest in Grace Callwood. If an activist is a person who campaigns to bring about social change, then Grace is campaigning for joy and happiness through her service. In fact, it is clear that joy *is* her activism. She is not the type of activist who campaigns for a policy change or holds a protest sign. A more just society, to Grace, will be a more joyful one.

"I have always loved making people happy, even just my friends and my family," Grace says. "Making people laugh, making people happy, random compliments, and just small things like that always bring me joy. So bringing that to kids who need it the most is something that I work for."

I can't help but wonder, How does Grace move toward joy? How does a seven-year-old with a cancer diagnosis find joy in playing cards in the hospital? If I'm being honest, joy is not always my default. I have often struggled to find joy, especially during challenging circumstances. In moments like these I understand why Jesus said that we as adults must change and become like little children (Matthew 18:3). Children appear to possess joy more easily than adults do. In this instance, Grace, in her youth, seems to be an expert in finding joy.

In her article "Joy Is an Act of Resistance: How Celebration Sustains Activism," Ingrid Fetell Lee writes that joy creates unity, disrupts expectations, promotes resilience, and gives rise to hope. Grace seeks to bring individuals and communities together through her service. She disrupts the expectation that there is an age limit on effecting sustainable change. Grace was resilient in persevering through illness, and she focused what little energy she had on bringing happiness to others. Grace has given rise to hope for thousands of people far and wide, including me.

We must hold on to our joy in the way we cling to hope. Resistant joy is not based on circumstances; rather, it denies challenging circumstances any right to dictate our emotions.

Of course we must be aware of our emotional ebbs and flows: a range of emotions makes us fully human. Yet we can still exert a level of free will even over our emotions. We can choose to have joy. Grace has given rise to hope in me—hope that joy can be found in the everyday, mundane things of life that we often take for granted.

By Serving Others, We Heal Ourselves

When Grace had cancer, the surgeries and treatments wiped the strength from her body. But even with the little energy she had, she served. "To heal means to make whole," writes professor Peter Northouse. "Servant leaders care about the personal well-being of their followers." Even when she was in the hospital, Grace could not help but think of other kids who were sick and how she might help them. That compassionate insight continues in her work today. Through her foundation, The We Cancerve Movement, almost every project description begins with an empathetic acknowledgment of what sick or disadvantaged youth may be experiencing:

> Imagine lying on a beach; the sand warm from the mid-day sun; the smell of salt water and fresh air; the sound of waves lapping against the shore. What a relaxing time. Who doesn't enjoy going to the beach? Unfortunately, children with some life-threatening illnesses can't go to the beach. That's why The We Cancerve Movement, Inc. brings the beach to them with our "Beach in a Bucket."
>
> Chemo treatments can be long and boring so We Cancerve donates 'Books & Buddies' to help young children pass the hours of infusions.

Finding [an Easter] basket full of treats, toys, and spring clothes is the experience [the] We Cancerve founder remembers from her childhood; that is, until she almost missed the opportunity because she was hospitalized really close to Easter. It was from her experience—at age seven—that she realized that Easter treats can be received just about anywhere including a hospital room. So, she created the Eggstra Special Easter bagskits project to bring happiness to homeless, sick and foster children.

Grace's main concern is the personal well-being of those she serves. She is attuned to their needs and creates initiatives to meet those needs. Writer and theologian Henri Nouwen would refer to Grace as a "wounded healer." In his book *The Wounded Healer*, he asks, "How can wounds become a source of healing?" He goes on to suggest that healing can take place through hospitality. To Nouwen, hospitality is a healing power. Through service and hospitality, our pain can become a transformative power for someone else. He writes, "Hospitality is the virtue that allows us to break through the narrowness of our own fears and to open our houses to the stranger, with the intuition that salvation comes to us in the form of a tired traveler."

Grace was once one of those tired travelers. She has turned into the one who opens the door to the stranger—the one who seeks to bring salvation through the hope of joy. Through her, I have learned that even if I am wounded, I can heal others even as I myself am healed.

Maintain a Spirit of Learning

Grace mentions the importance of what she refers to as "a spirit of learning." She says it is important to be able to receive feedback from other people. She is extremely self-aware. "I have to understand how other people view me despite me just knowing myself," Grace says. "Being a leader means taking inventory over yourself."

This spirit of learning is another aspect of servant leadership. Leaders should be aware and attuned to the environment and context they serve. This includes personal awareness and understanding oneself within the larger context. Grace frequently reflects on how she can grow and become a better person from every life circumstance with which she is presented. She approaches her relationships and encounters with others assuming she can learn something from each one.

Grace's spirit of learning is also an indication of her humility. Servant leaders are humble by nature, willing to put others' needs above their own. Humility is who Grace is. Humility is evidenced in her character and in her lifestyle. Her life has encouraged me to stop thinking of humility as confined to one instance or one lesson; instead, I can take on the mindset of humility and integrate it into my existence. Part of that humble mindset is this spirit of continual learning. We should always strive to grow, learn, and evolve, no matter how many academic degrees we have or how far along we are in our career. We will always have more to learn. A spirit of learning means allowing yourself to become a student of all that life entails. Every moment becomes a teachable one.

Happiness as Hope

In 2019, Grace spoke about her cancer journey to her congregation. Honest and vulnerable, she shared her struggle and how her faith in God helped her through it.

As she stepped to the pulpit and greeted the listeners, she said, "It is indeed a good morning. In fact, it is a great morning, because I am still alive." The congregation stood and applauded before she could continue. Then she said, "Cancer is a nasty, terrible disease that no one, and certainly no child, should ever have to face. I wish we lived in a world where cancer was a thing of the past."

Grace went on to share her story, including the painful moments and times in which she had felt like giving up. "I remember about five weeks into chemo. I squeezed [out] as much energy as my pale, limp, thin seven-year-old frame could and barely opened my eyes. I told my mom, 'I can't take this anymore. I can't hold on.'" Yet Grace did hold on. She endured her own suffering and emerged to help other young people through their pain and struggles.

Later that same year, Grace was named one of CNN's "Young Wonders" in a ceremony honoring young people creating a better world. On the night Grace was recognized and celebrated for her work with The We Cancerve Movement, she sat in the audience and beamed with joy as the young celebrity host, Caleb McLaughlin, introduced her life and work. "While she was fighting cancer, she got an idea to bring happiness to kids in tough situations," he said. "She delivers fun baskets to them in the hospital, started a boutique to give kids in foster care a free shopping experience, and launched a summer camp for those experiencing homelessness."

The audience also got to watch Grace in action. A short video showed her as an everyday teenager: skateboarding with her friends, learning in class, playing in the school marching band. The video also gave a glimpse into her personal journey after being diagnosed with cancer. "What I learned during my journey is that you can make your own happiness even in the midst of bad situations," she said in the film. "There will always be an opportunity to bring happiness to other people."

Once the video was over, Kelly Ripa, who was hosting the event along with Anderson Cooper, encouraged Grace to share some good news with the crowd. Confident and smiling from ear to ear, Grace said, "After being five years in remission, on February 7, I was declared cancer-free!" Grace was not only cancer-free—she was cured. Like her church congregation had done just a few months before, the crowd erupted into applause. The camera panned to her mother, T'Jae, who was wiping away tears.

Grace Callwood has fought the good fight, finished a difficult race, and kept the faith (2 Timothy 4:7). She is not just a CNN Young Wonder; she is a wonder and a hero to us all.

MOBILIZING FOR CHANGE
THE ADAPTIVE LEADERSHIP OF JAYCHELE NICOLE SCHENCK

Being able to use my platform for something
that is so much bigger than me is so amazing.
–Jaychele Nicole Schenck, co-founder and executive director,
Gen Z: We Want to Live

❧

Jaychele Schenck and Isabella James Indellicati first connected via social media through a mutual friend. They had similar interests, including a desire to bring attention to social injustice in the United States. Their online connection eventually turned into a greater endeavor as the two began to dream about creating something big.

"We just said, 'Let's make an organization,'" Jaychele told me. They both had the passion and the drive, and Jaychele had the training, experience, and connections that would help get the organization's first peaceful protest off the ground. Jaychele and Isabella announced the start of their new movement, Gen Z: We Want to Live, as well as their first protest, during a press conference on June 12, 2020. Jaychele spoke passionately about her anger at the injustice of Black lives being taken by police violence. "The youth are fed up," she said from a podium. "It is time for Rhode Island youth to take a stand."

While this was Jaychele's first time planning a protest, she had enough prior experience in event planning and mobilizing to formulate a strategic plan. She and Isabella used their personal social-media followings for engagement and marketing. In addition to the press conference, she remembers, "I was on the radio a couple of times, doing everything to get the word out." Just five days after their first announcements on social media and radio, 1,500 people gathered for the June 14 protest.

"People are paying attention now!" she screamed into a bullhorn at the rally. "They are listening to us now whether they want to or not! They have no choice but to sit at home and watch us or be here and protest with us or fight with us!" People surrounded her, clapping and cheering in agreement.

The protest came in the wake of the murder of George Floyd by police that sparked a national outcry. Under Jaychele's leadership, the crowd marched from Burnside Park in Providence, Rhode Island, to the State House. The group then staged a "die-in," lying down as if dead in the streets outside Providence Place Mall. They lay on the ground for 8 minutes and 46 seconds, the amount of time a Minneapolis police officer had knelt on the neck of George Floyd. "Black lives matter!" Jaychele exclaimed. The interracial and intergenerational crowd shouted the same phrase back repeatedly. People held signs and held up cell phones to capture the moment in pictures and videos.

"Black lives have mattered since all of you were born, since before I was born. We want to live! We are fighting for our lives!" Jaychele exclaimed. She is bold and passionate. When leading protests, she shouts as though her life literally depends on the words that come out of her mouth.

Gen Z: We Want to Live is a youth-led movement with a mission to fight for Generation Z "through youth advocacy and political influence, by building a coalition of skilled young activists." The name is straightforward, and urgent. When thinking about what to call their nonprofit, Jaychele says, the name came to them naturally. "I started thinking, what are things that Gen Zers all have in common? We all have dealt with tragedies like school shootings and race-based violence and climate change. What do we want to do? We all want to live." Jaychele goes on to say, "It is time for us to heal what we have inherited from the generations before us."

In a BuzzFeed article titled "Generation Free Fall," college student Hailey Modi echoes this sentiment. "I've noticed that in slightly older generations like millennials that there was some hope, but that was taken away through 9/11 and throughout the 2008 recession," Modi writes. "For Gen Z, that hope was never there. We grew up in a world where things have already gone terribly wrong and our lives are just preparing for the worst."

Jaychele remains focused on getting the organization to a national level. She wants them to be the next March for Our Lives, with youth-led chapters in multiple cities and states. In June 2020, the organization's website announced their first batch of policy initiatives, which include the implementation of a culturally relevant curriculum in the educational system; diversification of the educational workforce; abolishment of private prisons; putting police through independent training, racial bias testing, simulation training; and removing police from schools; and specialized service departments made accessible through 911.

In an email that went out to supporters on July 11, 2020, Jaychele wrote,

> While some people are beginning to believe that the fight for liberation is over, and that a name change for appeasement is enough, that is far from the reality. The whole community is still fighting, and it does not look like the fight is ending anytime soon. We are going to take this movement national, and that starts by making our impact right here in Rhode Island. I am not satisfied until we make a difference nationally. I am not just fighting for myself. I am fighting for the thousands of communities and millions of girls like me that are currently impacted and will continue to be without your support. . . .
>
> The youth are counting on you.

No words could ring truer. Young Black girls like Jaychele who are stepping up as leaders are counting on us. We cannot let them down.

Launched into Activism

Jaychele's activism began in 2018, after the mass shooting at Marjory Stoneman Douglas High School, where Tyah-Amoy Roberts was a student. Jaychele was in eighth grade at the time. In the aftermath, Jaychele saw young leaders like Tyah emerging and was immediately inspired. She attended a March for Our Lives rally in Rhode Island, and there, she says, she felt compelled to speak. Her outspokenness then led her to give her first testimony before a legislative body.

"That testimony was for the judiciary committee for Rhode Island State Senate," she explains. "It was a hearing on two gun-control bills. I was testifying against two bills."

The more Jaychele tells me about her activism, the more intrigued I become by terms she uses, many of which I'm unfamiliar with, at least in this context. When I hear the word *testify*, I think of a person at church sharing about how God did something miraculous in their life. To me, *testimony* suggests a public declaration about a religious experience. "What do you mean when you say 'testify'?" I ask.

Testifying, Jaychele explains, means speaking on an important issue at a public hearing. "Testifying is normally when you are speaking about a bill. It is usually related to the law," she explains. In the space of one conversation, Jaychele becomes my teacher.

Gen Z: We Want to Live isn't the first organization Jaychele has founded. When she was twelve years old, she started one called Dear Girls POP (Peace, Love and Positivity). "I intended Dear Girls to be an organization against girl-on-girl bullying," she tells me. "That's not really where it ended up. It ended up being a women's empowerment organization focused on the wage gap and educational programs."

Jaychele says that initiative never really took off, but she is grateful for experiences like that when she was younger, because they propelled her to where she is today. While she thinks about the dissolution of the organization and what she considered a failure, I sit in admiration that a twelve-year-old had the where-withal to start one in the first place. Meanwhile, Jaychele laments that she could have done so much more.

In ninth grade she joined an organization called Young Voices that focuses on two sectors: community and policy work. She credits Young Voices with offering her some initial leadership training through workshops and programs. One program, called Hotshots, taught the youth public speaking. They would speak for one minute on a particular topic and then the audience would give them feedback.

The group also provided what Jaychele described as "community circles." When a national crisis occurred, community circles provided students a safe space to talk. She describes various games the group would play that helped with communication or helped young people develop their story. From there, Jaychele went to work.

In her time with Young Voices, Jaychele gravitated toward the policy work, and she mainly focused on gun control. "I started off doing minor community-building work, and from there I really became an activist." At a 2019 Wear Orange event in Providence, which advocated for a future free of gun violence, Jaychele recited a poem she had written.

As a youth, I have been told that activism is a hobby

As a youth, I have been told that I am not capable of influencing policy

As a youth, I have been told that gun violence is a
  grown-up issue

As a youth, I have been told to let the adults continue

As a youth, I have been told to wait my turn

And now it is my turn to be a thorn

In the side of the politicians that fail to realize

The sounds of the cries from the parents getting the
  phone call that their children have died . . .

As I listen to Jaychele talk about becoming a board member of Young Voices, doing event planning and fundraising, I stop her mid-sentence to clarify her age at the time. "Thirteen? Well . . ." She pauses to think. "No, fourteen. I was fourteen. It seems like so much longer ago than it actually is." I find myself slightly intimidated speaking to her, but in a good way. Her convictions exceed her age. It brings me joy to be in the company of such a determined young woman.

And as if all that weren't enough, on the side she has a management agency. "I manage fifteen local rap and R&B artists, all under the age of twenty-one," she tells me. I'm sure my face must show my amazement.

"Do you do that on your own?" I ask. She nods casually. I sit there dumbfounded for a moment, considering all the commitments of time and energy Jaychele has on her plate: from activism and advocacy work to managing music artists and keeping up with schoolwork.

The almost-sixteen-year-old now attends high school at the Metropolitan Career and Technical Center. She is a math genius, having skipped advanced algebra and geometry. At the time of our conversation, she has just finished pre-calculus and is going to be taking college math her junior year. Even though she excels at math, her favorite subject has always been history. By the time she finishes high school, Jaychele will have her associate degree as a result of attending an accelerated program that lets students earn high school and college credit simultaneously. Harvard, Yale, and Brown University are some of her top college choices.

Her mother, who has been listening to our conversation from a distance, jumps in: "From birth she has been a miracle—like a joy. Jaychele is doing amazing things, and I can't be prouder." Then she turns and looks at Jaychele. "You may be sixteen next month, but you're still my baby girl. You are still a teenager."

Mobilizing Leadership

"I feel like I am a natural-born leader," Jaychele says. Her unique confrontation of social issues reflects a distinct leadership model. Jaychele is a mobilizer. In leadership studies, mobilizing leaders are also known as adaptive leaders.

In his book *Leadership*, Peter Northouse defines adaptive leaders as those who "engage in activities that mobilize, motivate, organize, orient, and focus the attention of others." This sentence describes Jaychele to her core. She motivates and organizes. She orients and focuses the attention of others. She mobilizes.

When Jaychele and her friend Isabella rallied more than a thousand people to come together for the protest in June 2020, many people who attended had no idea that it had been organized by two teenaged girls. In fact, Jaychele and Isabella had come up with the idea for the protest only two weeks prior to the event. Gathering large groups of people can be a difficult feat. Mobilizing those same people to agree on a common purpose is even more challenging. Jaychele has been able to galvanize large groups for a common purpose, and she makes it look effortless.

Adaptive leadership is an approach that organizes people specifically to address change. Mobilizing leaders see a political opportunity and then create organizational processes and structures around that opportunity. They are also thoughtful and deliberate in their communication strategies.

Jaychele's leadership activities embody all three of these traits. As a youth activist and community organizer, her leadership extends beyond racial and cultural lines to mobilize people with diverse backgrounds. She focuses her energies on encouraging her community to grow amid the inevitable challenges of life. Jaychele inspires people by encouraging them to put justice and equity into action. Through her platform she has addressed youth violence, prison reform, racial injustice, and other social challenges. She maintains a balance between providing the solutions herself and inspiring others to find solutions.

Jaychele's mobilizing and adaptive leadership inspires others to facilitate change in their own lives. Northouse writes, "Similar to a physician, an adaptive leader uses his or her expertise or authority to serve the people by diagnosing their problems and prescribing solutions." Jaychele is a solution-oriented leader who does not focus only on problems. She looks to provide solutions to every social problem she tackles. Whether that's a problem she sees in her community or a problem in society, she is always thinking, "How can this be solved?"

Black Women as Mobilizing Leaders

Black women have been at the forefront of adaptive leadership for years. In *Black Women as Leaders*, Lori Latrice Martin writes,

"Black women who are engaged in the practice of adaptive leadership have, over time, mobilized one another to tackle the tough challenges of protecting their bodies, representations, agency, families, community, franchise and autonomy, while simultaneously working to dismantle racialized social systems."

Black women in the past who led the fight against oppression often modeled adaptive leadership. They mobilized to form solutions to address the plight of Black men and women. Journalist, activist, teacher, and anti-lynching crusader Ida B. Wells-Barnett was an exemplary adaptive leader. Through her journalism, Wells-Barnett mobilized public opinion against lynching. She was active in the women's suffrage movement, and she organized Black women to fight for equal rights within that same movement. Her legacy is that of a reformer whose activism centered on the ongoing struggle for liberation of oppressed people.

Septima Poinsette Clark was another adaptive leader whose mobilization played an integral role in voting and civil rights for Black Americans in the civil rights movement. Her activism centered on literacy and citizenship. She stressed that both were crucial to political, economic, and social power for the Black community. She created "citizenship schools," which taught more than 25,000 adults to read.

Wells-Barnett and Clark are just two examples of the many Black women of our past who rose up as mobilizing leaders. Through their leadership, Black women have used carefully chosen strategies to bring about social change in local and national endeavors.

Today, we do not have to look far for a model of Black adaptive leadership. Stacey Abrams is the quintessential mobilizing leader.

She also happens to be one of Jaychele's heroes. Jaychele beams when she talks about Abrams. "She is such an inspiration to me. She's such a huge personality in the best way possible and for the best reasons. Her presence speaks for her. She is so inspiring that whenever people see her or see what she has done, they immediately have a feeling of jumping into action."

The world knows Abrams as the voting-rights activist, lawyer, and politician who helped Georgia turn blue in the 2020 presidential election. For over ten years, she has fought voter suppression in Georgia. Her organization, Fair Fight, works to create awareness about voter suppression, educate people of color on voting rights, and create voter-protection teams across the state. Through her mobilization efforts, she has helped more than 800,000 people register as new voters in the state. The efforts of Abrams and other Black women during the 2020 presidential election are what led Vice President Kamala Harris to honor Black women in her speech after the election was called. "I want to speak directly to the Black women in our country," Harris tweeted after the election. "Thank you. You are too often overlooked, and yet are asked time and again to step up and be the backbone of our democracy. We could not have done this without you."

Black women leaders like Stacey Abrams and Jaychele are the backbone of our democracy. They mobilize to take on the tough challenges that disenfranchised communities face. They show us that resistance and activism come in different forms.

Jaychele's Leadership Wisdom

So, what do we learn when we look to Jaychele's style of mobilizing and adaptive leadership?

Believe in What You Fight For

"I'm not going to tell you to fight for what you believe in, because you are doing that by being here today," Jaychele told a group of people calling for gun-violence reduction in 2019. "I'm going to tell you to believe in what you fight for. That belief will push you through the hard experiences of activism. It will allow you to have faith in the future and what it holds."

I often think about the question "What is your why?" as it relates to my own life. While I am more self-assured in my calling now than when I was an adolescent, I still find myself having to revisit the question of what fuels that sense of purpose.

"The younger kids are the reason why I continue to fight. What's their name?" Jaychele asks.

"Alpha Gen," I respond. This new generation comprises the children of millennials, born beginning in 2010.

"Yeah, I'm fighting for them," she tells me. "And at the same time, I'm fighting for the people who came before me who didn't get to see justice."

Jaychele believes in what her predecessors stood for, and she believes in the essential goodness of younger generations to make our world a better place. Jaychele is fighting from a liminal space: both honoring our past and prophetically hoping for our future. She caused me to ask myself: Why do I fight for the voices of Black women and girls? Why am I so passionate about centering their lives and experiences?

Watching Jaychele, I realize I am fighting for the dignity of our humanity. I am fighting for those of us who continually go overlooked in this world. I am fighting for our voices to be heard. I am fighting for our existence.

It is not just enough to fight; we must continually revisit the reason *why* we fight and believe in what we're fighting for.

Go Ahead and Get Emotional

"You don't like me because I'm a loud Black woman, and I don't care!"

Jaychele once proclaimed these words at a protest rally against gun violence. She explains to me that she was surprised when her words appeared above an article about the protest in a local newspaper. Jaychele was a bit disturbed by the editors' choice for the headline. It seemed like a convenient line to place next to her picture—convenient in its reliance on the stereotype of the angry and loud Black woman. The audacity of that decision could have made her even more angry. On the other hand, Jaychele says, she doesn't really mind if people see her that way. She knows anger is part of the work, and she's not afraid of her emotions.

Jaychele's response reminds me of an interview with activist Tamika Mallory, in which she spoke about the stereotype of Black women being angry. "It is my truth that I am angry," Mallory said. "I'm frustrated. I'm angry. I am a pretty smart girl, and my time is being dedicated to fighting against racists and bigotry and fascism because we're trying to fight for future generations. So, hell yeah, we're angry."

Both Tamika and Jaychele are bold and unapologetic about their emotions. Instead of shying away from the angry Black woman trope, both women have found a way to lean in. They acknowledge that our anger is real, our anger is justified, and our anger is human. And they know that leaders should not have to withdraw from their real emotions.

Unfortunately, those in leadership often feel obliged to suppress their emotions for the greater good. While on tour for her book *Becoming*, Michelle Obama once described the moments after the 2016 inauguration when she and President Barack Obama boarded the Marine One helicopter. She said she sobbed for thirty minutes and it wasn't because she was sad to leave. Her tears were the release of eight years of trying to do everything perfectly. For eight years in the public eye, she felt she had to maintain emotional control. Yet despite her efforts, unfair headlines still targeted Michelle Obama, labeling her as angry and mean.

For Black women and girls in leadership, the suppression of anger in particular is a constant source of internal conflict. Yet Jaychele reminds us that we need our anger to help fuel us for the challenges leadership brings. We need our anger, and we need all of our emotions. We can experience this spectrum of emotions and still be strong leaders.

Strive for a Higher Self

"I believe in God, but I also tend to focus on my higher self," Jaychele tells me at one point. Our society is obsessed with public images, branding, beauty, and body image. These, however, will not lead us to our higher selves. In order to connect to the divine essence that God placed inside each of us, our focus must turn inward. Spiritual counselor and author Aletheia Luna describes the higher self as "your True Nature: it is your wise, unconditionally loving, creative, Whole, and eternal inner Center. Deep down, we all carry a certain level of resonance with these words. We recognize that there is something mysterious within us, something sacred."

All of us should strive to become the best version of ourselves. To do so, we must commit to doing internal work. This might be the hardest work we face—harder, even, than mobilizing and organizing and inspiring others. When we aim to transform our inner selves, we confront difficult parts of ourselves that we typically avoid. When we commit to the internal work, we face our ego, our insecurities, and the emptiness that comes with the undertaking. But on the other end of this challenging work we will awaken to our most whole, balanced, and peaceful selves.

I wondered why Jaychele does not seem to need the validation of her peers or other people. The more we talked, the more I realized that any person like Jaychele who strives to be their highest self has evolved to a place of internal peace that is not swayed by outside influences. To Jaychele, being a leader begins with learning to trust her own voice and leadership.

Mobilizing for Change

In late 2020, Black Lives Matter Rhode Island awarded Jaychele and her organization the Harriet Tubman Activism Award. She considers it a passing of the torch. In an older social media post, Jaychele reflected on all the hard work that led to the success of Gen Z: We Want to Live: "This movement brought me to tears. If you told 12-year-old me this, she'd laugh in your face. Being able to use my small platform for something that is so much bigger than me is so amazing." No matter what the road ahead looks like, Jaychele persists. With the tenacious spirit of her inspiration, Stacey Abrams, Jaychele fights for a more equal and just society. "I am not just fighting for myself, she says. "I am fighting for the thousands of communities and millions of girls like me."

Several months after they started their organization, Jaychele and Isabella taught a series of workshops on youth activism called "Generation of Change." The ten-day class culminated with the youth in attendance creating chapters of Gen Z: We Want to Live. Jaychele and Isabella also posted a query on the Gen Z website, inviting anyone who was interested in starting a chapter to fill out an application.

"People just started applying, and we ended up having a couple of chapters," Jaychele says. "It ended up working out really well for Election Day, because we were able to have voter registrations across the country for Gen Z youth who were able to register. That was really exciting."

This is exactly what the two leaders envisioned when they began. In less than one year since Jaychele and Isabella first brainstormed the name for their new organization, they have active chapters of Gen Z: We Want to Live in Texas, Pennsylvania, Maryland, Missouri, Connecticut, Massachusetts, and California. The Gen Z Texas chapter is investigating how their schools are being affected by the pandemic. They are doing letter-writing campaigns to their governor and the state health department. The Gen Z Maryland and Missouri chapters are working on anti-redlining campaigns, which work against discriminatory practices that deny services to residents of certain areas because of their race. The California, Massachusetts, and Connecticut chapters are in the beginning stages of organizing. Regardless of each group's direction, Jaychele's role is to train and support them in preparing for the work at hand. "If they want to do policy work, then we will do policy workshops with them to make sure they're ready to write policy and make connections and presentations."

Again, the influence of Stacey Abrams is apparent in Jaychele's zeal for training and mobilizing. Jaychele is the mirror image of the Black women who engaged in mobilizing leadership and who came before her.

Even though she is busy in the moment, Jaychele looks forward to the future. "I was planning on staying here in Rhode Island for college and getting things situated so that I can run for office pretty soon," she tells me. She says she wants to run for state senate while she's in college, with plans to run for US Senator by the time she is thirty. "There are currently no Black women in the Senate [since Senator Kamala Harris became Vice President Kamala Harris], and I want to run," she tells me.

Hopefully, by the time Jaychele arrives in the Senate, she will be welcomed into the company of many other Black women senators ushering all of us into a new era of change.

6

SHIFTING THE NARRATIVE
THE ENVIRONMENTAL ETHICS OF AMARA IFEJI

There is not a single narrative or a single story of an individual who belongs in the outdoors. The outdoors is not just a place for an individual who looks this way or has these resources. It is a human right.
–Amara Ifeji, environmental justice activist

❧

██ I started off exploring in the dirt, and up until [now at] eighteen years old, I was still playing in the dirt," Amara laughs. As a child, Amarachukwu Ifeji loved to play outdoors in Maine, which is known for its rivers, lakes, and wildlife forests.

"I think that pretty much holds for all environmental stewards or climate justice activists—that call or connection to place with the environment," she says. Already, Amara has made a significant impact as a climate and racial justice activist. A profile piece for a daily newspaper in Maine states: "As she graduates from Bangor High School, Nigerian-born Amara Ifeji leaves behind a legacy of scientific achievement and social change." Those words summarize the impact she has had in her small corner of the country.

"There are only two seasons in Maine: winter and preparing for winter," Amara tells me. "We're currently in preparing for winter. It is a bit cloudy today, but the sun is peaking through. Climate change is a thing. We have hit 100 [degrees]. We've only done that four times in history."

I admit that I don't know much about Maine, but in conversing with Amara, I can sense her deep-seated love for her home state. "Maine has afforded me opportunities," she says thoughtfully. "I want to be a part of that progressive change to make the state I love a better place to live, work, and raise a family in. I never thought I would say that."

Amara spent most of her adolescence wanting to leave Maine. Maine is almost 95 percent white. Black people make up less than 2 percent of the population, with other races and ethnicities falling into similar percentages. Amara has spent years feeling disappointed in the slow progress the state has made with regard to racism and other issues around equity and inclusion. In a piece about the legacy of racism in Maine, high school teacher and opinion writer Laura Fralich writes, "In Maine's schools, Black students continue to speak out against the racist abuse and harassment that they are subjected to, as well as the inaction of school administrations. In addition, the recent protests against police brutality have highlighted the fact that in cities across the state, Black people are two to four times more likely to be arrested by police than white people."

Amara is one of those young students fighting for racial justice in New England. In a video for Connecticut Public Radio, Amara spoke of her experience as a young Black woman growing up in Maine. "In Maine there are many sundown towns, where I just really cannot be found after a certain time," she says. Sundown towns are all-white communities that discriminate against Black people and other people of color by using unjust laws, threats of violence, and other practices to intimidate and discourage them from driving into their neighborhoods after sundown. Amara continues, "Those are the kinds of things that my mother was fearful of [when we moved here]—people who harbored hate for people who look like me."

Despite her desire to leave, Amara sees herself as helping to usher progressive change into Maine. "Now that I have grown, I have come to understand that my place is here. That's where God has called me to. Of all the states that my mother pursued an education, she decided on Maine."

Amara was born in Nigeria in 2001. Her family moved to the United States in 2004 and first lived in Maryland, but they eventually moved to Maine. Her parents experienced professional and educational setbacks in their new home country. Though Amara's father was a lawyer in Nigeria, when they arrived in America, he had to attend school again because his education and experience did not afford him the same opportunities here as they had there. Similarly, while Amara's mother held two degrees that she had received in Nigeria, many of the credits she had earned did not transfer when the family uprooted and moved to the United States. Amara's mother is now a practicing pharmacist at a hospital in Bangor, and her father is working on his dissertation for a doctorate in business administration.

Amara calls her mother her "primary motivator" in life. "I aspire to be like my mother," she says, beaming with pride. "She wanted to show her children that they can be anything they want in this world with education. Education is that path that will see you through."

Racism on Playgrounds

Two weeks after nine-year-old Amara first moved to Maine, she played a game on the playground and won. At first, she was elated, but that excitement faded after a boy bitterly called her a "ni**er monkey."

"I didn't even know how to act," she recalls painfully. "I think I just ran away. I think I was embarrassed. I was so angry. I think that I . . ." Amara pauses, struggling to find the words. "I wasn't embarrassed about what that kid said. I was embarrassed because I was Black. I was embarrassed because I was only one of a few Black kids at my four-hundred-plus elementary school. That started a cycle of me struggling to come to terms with the fact that I am something that is very apparent—being Black."

It was such a pivotal moment for Amara that she wrote her college entrance essay on the horrifying experience: "Ni**er. My first encounter with this word was during an intense battle of four-square. In the courtyard of my elementary school, a crowd gathered to watch the heated game. The ball whizzed back and forth between my opponent and I. Swiftly, I struck the ball with a force he could not return. I beamed with joy: in all my nine years, never before had I secured the coveted fourth square. But my smile vanished as he looked at me and yelled, 'Ni**er monkey!' Shocked, tears filled my eyes as I lost myself in a sea of white."

Many of the Black girls I have talked to and interviewed over the years have similar stories of encountering racism on the playgrounds of their childhood. And twenty years ago, on a playground in suburban East Brunswick, New Jersey, I experienced an incident that was strikingly similar to the one Amara describes. I was only one of a handful of Black students among one thousand students at my elementary school. Just a few weeks after school started, I was playing on the playground when a boy who was white came over to play with me. His friend stopped him and told the boy, "We don't play with ni**ers." The boy looked at his friend and said, "You're not supposed to say that." The two then turned and walked away. I stood there alone, feeling confused and ashamed. The hurt and humiliation of that moment burrowed so deep into my consciousness that even now, as an adult, that memory sticks with me.

For both Amara and me, these incidents started unhealthy cycles of self-hatred. Amara says she started straightening her hair and finding ways to try to lighten her skin and slenderize her nose. She is aware now of how her self-hatred was connected to the hatred that had clearly been instilled in the white boy. "In hindsight, it makes me sad that a nine-year-old grew up in an environment where they knew the weight of that word, and what it could have against me," she says.

As Amara moved through the school system, she continued to observe inequity and discrimination in various forms. "I liked certain aspects of my school. I valued my education. I liked my teachers," she recounts. "But there were a lot of things about my high school that I did not like. I did not like how they sweep racism, transphobia, misogyny, harassment all under the [rug]. They don't acknowledge it. They paint the person reporting on these incidents to be the person in the wrong."

Amara was one of a group of students interviewed by a *Bangor Daily News* reporter for an article about racism. The piece highlighted the experiences of Bangor High School students who described a hostile and racist educational climate: constantly hearing the N-word from their peers, seeing the confederate flag on display, and receiving offensive comments and jokes. Amara described the toll that contentious environment took on her mental health: "I was tired of walking through the halls and hearing the N-word. No form of punishment, no form of discipline. It made me feel extremely undervalued as a student."

Throughout her high school career, Amara actively worked to create change by leading racial advocacy efforts, which eventually led to policy change at her school. She has also spoken openly about her experiences before the Bangor City Council and the school board. After a presentation to the school board, she organized the first diversity and inclusion panel discussion at her high school, which focused on sharing a space to discuss issues of discrimination at the school. In September 2019, Amara launched the Multicultural Student Union, a group of BIPOC (Black, Indigenous, people of color) students who convene once a week to discuss their lived experiences and issues they face at school. She also founded the Minority Student Union, which creates a space for all students to work on developing cultural competence and creating change.

"My high school experience should not have been shrouded in racism or injustice or me feeling uncomfortable in my learning environment," Amara says. "Our motto at my school is 'Academic excellence for all.' That can't be the case unless there is an equitable, inclusive learning environment for everyone—and that does not just mean race but in every single regard."

For Amara, her identity as a BIPOC individual living in Maine intersects with her passion for racial justice advocacy. At the same time, her environmental interests are inextricably linked to her experience of growing up in Maine, a state full of vast forests, wetlands, mountains, and other natural landscapes.

Climate Activism

Amara didn't receive much formal environmental education in school beyond the basics about ecosystems and the outdoor Maine landscape. As a result, she sought out opportunities to learn on her own. In high school, she attended an event with the Maine Environmental Changemakers Network that shifted her perspective from a science-based one to a social one. This was the beginning of her climate activism. At the Changemakers event, she learned about the disproportionate impact environmental exploitation has on marginalized communities. An intersection was forming, this one between her two passions of environmental activism and racial justice.

"I had my environmental action, and I had my racial justice work, but I kind of put them in two different boxes," Amara says. As we talk, she reflects on how these issues intersected not only with each other but with her upbringing. "I recognized things in my past in terms of socioeconomic status. That was a barrier to access that I had in terms of fostering a connection to the environment."

Amara talks to me about not being able to afford winter boots and snow pants, which meant she couldn't connect with her environment during the cold months. She recalls missing out on environmental outings because of expenses her family could not afford. She says the stigmas around Black people skiing or camping influenced her decision to not engage in any of those activities. And she mentions one significant barrier in particular: "My mother was very apprehensive of me going outside," she says, "especially at nighttime, because I am a Black individual and there is a stigma in the Black community around being outside, especially at night."

Black youth being afraid to walk outdoors in the evening is an intersectional environmental issue. The 2012 murder of seventeen-year-old Trayvon Martin, who was shot while walking through a neighborhood on the way back from a convenience store, underscored this fear. Deemed "suspicious" by another man in the community, Trayvon was guilty of nothing more than being Black and walking with his hood up in the evening.

"If I did not recognize that there was a link between social justice and environmental issues, I don't really think that I would be in this work," Amara says. "These aren't two different things that I am working toward making better. They are one."

This two-pronged issue is known as environmental racism. Given the environmental racism Amara has seen around her, she is committed to the work of environmental equity. MobilizeGreen, a nonprofit organization focused on jumpstarting green careers for diverse students, writes: "Environmental equity describes a country, or world, in which no single group or community faces disadvantages in dealing with environmental hazards, disasters, or pollution." Large segments of the population are disproportionately affected by environmental barriers. Amara strives to be a changemaker within the world of environmental activism and environmental equity.

"The environmental sector is extremely white," Amara says. "It is extremely cisgender, straight, white male–dominated. And those who are typically affected by things like natural disasters and environmental phenomena are BIPOC individuals. One in three African American individuals live within thirty miles of a coal plant. That is called environmental racism if I ever did hear it."

Environmental justice scholar Vanessa Fabien writes something similar: "Historically, the environmental debate has highlighted the experiences of privileged white men who possessed the social, political and economic capital to advance their particular agendas in the environmental discourse. As a result, the dominant historiography in American environmental history has marginalized the experiences of African Americans, Native Americans and other communities of color."

Eventually, Amara evolved from a young woman merely interested in environmental issues to a climate justice activist. "I attended some climate strikes, other environmental protests as well," she says. "I became more active in facilitation at different conferences. That's when I started investing more time into gaining more knowledge."

Amara was involved in the Bangor High School STEM (science, technology, engineering, and math) program for much of her school career. There she engaged issues like water quality and heavy-metal pollution. She participated in an independent research project that focused on the Flint, Michigan, water crisis and trying to resolve heavy-metal contamination in drinking water.

Later Amara became president of the Stormwater Management and Research Team (SMART). SMART is a youth-led water-quality management team that provides female students with opportunities to explore environmental STEM. There she worked weekly for almost a year to sample the Penobscot Watershed in order to ensure that the river was safe for recreational use. One of her most notable accomplishments was securing funding for the organization to provide programming for girls who were underrepresented in STEM. "The Summer Training Institute was particularly for girls of color and socioeconomically marginalized individuals as well, because seldom do you find those three groups of individuals in STEM."

Through the program, Amara led the students through field sampling, toured stormwater treatment facilities, and exposed them to pressing environmental issues. During the school year, she facilitated weekly meetings and personally mentored each member on a water-quality research project. The institute was a success, and a group of girls from the program received awards at the Maine State Science Fair due to the research they did on water quality.

Amara has also received accolades of her own. Her research, which focuses on the use of plants and fungi in the removal of heavy metals from water, secured her the Best of Category Award at the Regeneron International Science and Engineering Fair and a Top 300 Regeneron Science Talent Search National Award. For her work in environmental justice, she was presented with the Maine Environmental Education Association Student of the Year Award. Her research projects, which have won numerous awards, centered on methods of water purification in STEM. Amara is now a grassroots development coordinator with the Maine Environmental Changemakers Network, "a youth-led intergenerational network that connects young Mainers . . . from diverse backgrounds who are passionate about the environment with peer mentors, and established professional mentors, in the sector." As the grassroots development coordinator, Amara continues to advocate for intersectional climate justice solutions through various programs and initiatives.

"Through my work, I've led efforts to allow individuals, especially those from marginalized backgrounds, to recognize that the environment and the outdoors is not just a place for an individual who looks this way or has these resources. It is a human right."

Black Environmental Ethics

Land has historically been an important part of Black people's identity and spirituality. Our African ancestors believed that land was a gift from God. Because of this, they took great pride in the land and saw themselves as stewards of God's resources. Unfortunately, slavery forced our ancestors to work the American soil and build the infrastructure of this nation through sweat and blood with no reward. Rev. Dr. Heber Brown, founder and director of the Black Church Food Security Network, says, "The African American community has suffered so much from disconnection to the land." He goes on to assert that spirituality in the Black community was injured by this wickedness that took our land and divided our families. Through his network, Rev. Dr. Brown has found a way to reconnect the Black community to the land that was stripped from them.

Amara's passions reflect her deep spiritual connection with the environment. It is a homecoming of sorts, and a calling back to the land on which our ancestors toiled. One can sense this, not only in the passion for her work but in the continual state of gratitude she expresses for her physical surroundings. In an interview for Maine Public Radio with host Irwin Gratz, Amara tells him about the first time she visited Acadia National Park in Maine: "My first time going there, I remember driving up Cadillac Mountain and looking over the huge expanse and just falling in love with the beautiful landscape before me. And I think that's really when—I was maybe ten years old or so—I made a commitment to myself, as well as to Mother Nature, to protect her, so that generations to come would be able to really engage and explore the outdoors, just as I had done that day."

Amara expresses a similar commitment and spiritual connection to her surroundings as did MaVynee Oshun Betsch. Betsch, an early twentieth-century environmentalist and activist, was known as "the Beach Lady" because she was the unofficial historian of American Beach in Jacksonville, Florida. Betsch was born in Jacksonville in 1935 and spent the early part of her life traveling as an opera singer. Later in life, when she returned to Florida, she began her passionate advocacy for protection of the environment. Eventually she moved to American Beach and directed her attention toward the preservation of the beach. Betsch saw the beach as a significant part of Black history.

In one interview, MaVynee Betsch spoke about her spiritual experience at the beach: "Many nights I just sit on the beach . . . it's as if all my troubles go out with the next tide. One of the things that I love here. It's such a spiritual high. Then there are the nights. The strange, strange nights, when you're sitting on that beach and somewhere deep in our own memory, psychic or whatever you want to call it, one can almost hear those chains." She is, of course, referencing the chains of captive Africans brought to America as part of the transatlantic slave trade.

MaVynee Betsch and Amara both testify to their spiritual connection with the land and their sense of responsibility to protect it. Betsch's mission to preserve and protect the history of American Beach resulted in the opening of the American Beach Museum nine years after her 2005 death. Betsch was an advocate for many other environmental causes too. She was a member of sixty environmental organizations and a life member of ten. At the end of her life, Betsch gave away her entire fortune to environmental causes. Both MaVynee Betsch, as a Black woman environmental activist of our past, and Amara Ifeji, as a young Black woman environmental activist of our present, teach us that we have a sacred and ethical responsibility to protect the land.

Ethical Leadership

At the end of her senior year, Amara was awarded a $5,000 Mainely Character Scholarship sponsored by 100+ Women Who Care Southern Maine. The scholarship honors leaders who exemplify four aspects of character: integrity, concern, responsibility, and courage. These are among the many distinct qualities I have been able to witness in Amara's personhood and leadership. These are qualities that demonstrate the kind of ethical leader she is.

Ethical leadership is a form of leadership that is guided by ethical values, beliefs, and principles. An ethical person values honesty and integrity and lives by the principle of trying to do the right thing. Amara is an ethical leader. Her values guide her in both her personal and her professional life. She lives in a constant state of concern for others, for her home state of Maine, and for the larger world.

In *Leadership: Theory and Practice*, Peter Northouse lists five principles of ethical leadership that reflect characteristics of leaders like Amara: (1) ethical leaders respect others, (2) ethical leaders serve others, (3) ethical leaders are just, (4) ethical leaders are honest, and (5) ethical leaders build community. Amara's ethical code is made evident in an interview with *Future Focus*, a speaker series featuring Maine's youth climate-justice activists. Amara responds to a viewer's question about what it would take for one to become better at addressing social issues. She says, "In order to be in a place where not just one person feels comfortable but everyone in that work feels comfortable, one needs to get uncomfortable. I think one needs to look internally in their work and the things they do. What are your practices? Do they have equity within those practices? Are they formed thinking of not just one individual or one community but all individuals in all communities?"

In their book *Leading from the Emerging Future*, Otto Scharmer and Katrin Kaufer write, "We cannot transform the behavior of systems unless we transform the quality of attention that people apply to their actions within those systems, both individually and collectively." In order for unhealthy systems to change, people within those systems must change their own actions through consistent self-evaluation. Amara takes that one step further by suggesting that we must continually question whether our work is looking out for the good of everyone. If it is not, then we cannot be comfortable. Visual artist and activist Lilla Watson once said, "If you have come here to help me you are wasting your time; but if you have come because your liberation is bound up with mine, then let us work together." Amara lives by these principles.

Amara's Leadership Wisdom

Amara's conversation is full of insight and counsel. Perhaps a mix of her life experiences and ethical leadership has propelled her to such wisdom.

We Can Be Critical of the Things We Love

Amara loves her home state of Maine. At the same time, she expresses critical perspectives of Maine and its issues, whether concerning environmentalism, racism, or other discriminatory facets. Amara boldly speaks out against these problems not out of malevolence but out of love and concern. She holds those same sentiments about her high school. She has been vocal about her problems with the administration's approach to discrimination and injustice. Yet at the same time, Amara affirms that she sees progress and change happening incrementally. She will continue to push for that change so the school can live up to its objective of being a safe space for all its students.

The word *critical* often has negative connotations. A critical person finds fault and judges harshly. However, criticism also involves "skillful judgment as to truth, merit." Amara's critical gaze at her surroundings demonstrates this sort of skillful judgment. Her critique of racial and environmental inequity involves speaking truth to power, and it is rooted in her experiences. In that sense, she is a critical theorist: one who challenges power structures and who is motivated, according to Ashley Crossman, by "a social theory oriented toward critiquing and changing society as a whole." Critical theorists also challenge power structures: Amara has challenged everyone from her school administration to state government. Reasonably, we cannot all be critical theorists;

117

however, we can learn from the basic philosophy of frequently reflecting on and assessing the spaces in which we spend our time. From Amara, I learn that both loving something and holding it accountable grow out of the same impulse.

I have often heard people say things like "If you don't like it here, then just leave." But just because a person highlights issues and actively seeks to bring about change, that does not mean that same person wants to abandon that space. We can remain where we are in love, while holding the people, places, and things we love accountable.

Everyone Belongs

Amara operates with the philosophy of life that everyone belongs. "There is not [just] a single narrative, there's not a single person, there's not a single story of an individual who belongs in the outdoors. Everyone has a place in the environment," she says. She believes not only that everyone has a place in the environment, but that everyone has a place in our society and world at large. Amara's earlier experiences of racism were not only discriminatory; they also undermined her personal sense of belonging. In a society in which Black girls like Amara experience marginalization for both their race and their gender, finding and creating secure spaces where they are valued is essential to their well-being. Belonging is an emotional need for acceptance and support. Belonging is a fundamental desire for human connection.

Belonging is emotional, but it is also inherently spiritual, because through it we connect to our purpose and identity. When a person feels they belong, they're able to navigate the existential questions of life, such as "What is the meaning of life?"; "How do I fit in?"; and "What's my purpose?" It is our responsibility to foster a sense of belonging among the people around us.

We can help others feel that they belong with a few simple strategies. In her article "Helping Students Feel Like They Belong," author Mary Beth Hewitt suggests ways to create belongingness among students. She asked students how they knew they belonged to a group. Their responses ranged from "They include me," to "They know my name," to "They take an interest in what is important to me," to "They listen to me." While these were student responses, I believe that they apply to all human beings.

Amara challenges us with similar ways of assessing our principles of belonging. Looking back to her interview with *Future Focus,* she offers questions we should contemplate:

- What are your practices?

- Do you have equity within those practices?

- Are your practices formed thinking of not just one individual or one community but all individuals in all communities?

Fostering belonging for those around us is no easy task, both because it is a continual process of self-assessment and because we might fail or make mistakes. However, Amara says we should lean into the discomfort of the process because it is a part of our commitment to the hard work.

See the Beauty in Everything

One of the more profound traits I noticed in Amara is her ability to see beauty in everything around her. Amara speaks as though she is in awe of nature. I have seldom noticed the small details about the environment I live in, let alone taken the time to appreciate them. Yet every time Amara describes the landscape of Maine, she does so with careful intention and wonder. I also noticed that when she speaks of people, she goes beyond what may appear on the surface and affirms the goodness in all of us. She calls us to pay attention to those who are overlooked, underrepresented, or marginalized, and to see the worthiness and value in them as we do ourselves.

Because of Amara's capacity to see this beauty, she holds on to the belief that the society around her can be better. She combats racism and misogyny from the perspective that those issues should not exist, and she believes that people are fully capable of rising above hate and discrimination. Amara believes that even the worst people can become better, kinder human beings. She approaches her environmental activism from the belief that our society can maintain an eco-friendly and sustainable approach. She knows that our environment is capable of flourishing if we take care of it.

Amara teaches us that not all of life is perfect, but it is beautiful. She reminds us to pay attention to the small details. She challenges us to look for the worth and value of all people. By deliberately seeing the beauty around us, we may find the peace we need to live more meaningful and grateful lives.

Shifting the Narrative

On the cusp of young adulthood, Amara is only just beginning. Her wisdom, advocacy, and activism have been instrumental in effecting change in the state of Maine. Most recently she was awarded the Global North American Environmental Education

30 Under 30 International Award—one of only six people under thirty in the United States recognized for their leadership in environmental education. She was also selected as a National Geographic Young Explorer, joining an international cohort of young world-changers who are charged with developing solutions to pressing problems in their communities. As journalist Bill Nemitz wrote, she is "changing the world, one small corner at a time."

Amara is now attending Northeastern University, majoring in politics, philosophy, and economics with a minor in environmental studies. While school and other opportunities may take her far from home, she holds Maine in her heart and can see herself possibly pursuing a career in politics in the state House of Representatives. "I know that I want to pursue politics. I think the ultimate goal will be the US Senate," she ruminates. Amara believes that she can achieve whatever she sets her sights on, because of those who came before her.

"I started to see people like AOC [US Representative Alexandria Ocasio-Cortez]. I started to see people like [Vice President] Kamala Harris or [Speaker of the House] Nancy Pelosi. I started to see all of these women and BIPOC women attaining high leadership positions, and I thought to myself: if they can do it, I can do it."

Amara has come a long way not only in her work but in her evolving sense of identity. She wrote about this evolution in her honest, heartbreaking, and powerful college essay referenced earlier: "I came from a community where I was outwardly indistinguishable from my peers. In Maryland, I was just another girl whose kinky-coily hair defied gravity, whose skin was kissed by the sun, and whose bilingual tongue often mixed up words and phrases. This became especially evident upon my move to Maine. My dark skin, large nose, and big lips were the antithesis to the fair skin and Eurocentric features of those in my new community. No longer was I just another Black girl. Now, I was *the* Black girl." Her negative experiences of discriminatory comments and treatment just confirmed those feelings.

But despite those circumstances, Amara has shifted the narrative about herself: "Although I still live in a sea of whiteness, instead of sinking below the surface, I am buoyant in my identity, jetting across the surface and making waves." By the time she graduated from high school, she was able to stand out in a different way, making an extraordinary name for herself in Maine and beyond.

THE HERO OF HER OWN STORY
THE PACESETTING OF KYNNEDY SIMONE SMITH

I seek to find the art in everything. Life is art, and when
we can create things through art that can connect, impact, heal, or
inspire–that is my ultimate goal for everything. To put art in everything. Art is life, and we learn from and adapt to it.
–Kynnedy Simone Smith, scholar, violinist, entrepreneur

❧

Before Kynnedy Simone Smith was even born, her mother
declared that she would be the child to break generational
curses in their family. Although Kynnedy's mother would raise
her as a single parent under difficult financial and personal circumstances, she dedicated her life to ensuring that her daughter
had every resource she needed to thrive.

Now a young woman looking back on her growing-up years, Kynnedy is inspired by her mother. "My mom really worked hard to make sure I had everything I need," Kynnedy reflects. "I want to be like my mother in the sense where I am able to sacrifice in order to support other people. She sacrificed her entire life in order to support me and her future family."

Her mother's love, sacrifice, and hard work paid off. Kynnedy is now an academic scholar, a classically trained violinist, the founder of several initiatives and organizations, and the recipient of multiple honors and awards. She is passionate about STEM, the arts, and matters of diversity and inclusion.

Despite her achievements, there have been times when people at her school (a predominantly white independent school) have told her to stop talking about her involvements because her accomplishments have made them feel bad. "It is a lot of pressure," she says, "but it's all good pressure. But it did fuel in me a sense of perfectionism at a young age. Every day I am always being told that I need to be five times better than everyone else, especially as a Black girl."

Her mature and soothing voice makes me forget that I'm speaking to a seventeen-year-old. Kynnedy is thoughtful and unassuming. As we talk, I find myself feeling proud of her even though I don't yet know her.

Originally from Shaker Heights, Ohio, Kynnedy grew up surrounded by Cleveland arts and culture. She took dance, music, and art classes throughout her childhood. She started playing the violin when she was just nine years old. In one interview, she explains what drew her to the violin: "My mother listened to a lot of jazz and instrumental music when I was little, so I instantly became fond of the many ways one can create music out of different instruments and sounds," she says. "When I was five, I first saw and heard a woman playing the violin at a community dinner. It was then that I told my mother that I wanted to play that instrument."

Kynnedy was given her first violin by her local Boys and Girls Club when she was in the fourth grade, and she joined her elementary school orchestra. Kynnedy is now a gospel jazz violinist with more than ten years of classical and contemporary music study under her belt. She has performed on both national and international stages.

"I want music to be something that I do for enjoyment and for healing purposes. I'm really big on music for healing." In the future she wants to be what she calls a "session musician": "Like basically I would be the person playing in the background," she says, "like when Beyoncé did Coachella and she had the violinist. I'd play for awards shows. In the back of soundtracks. Or pit-musician work for musicals."

"Your mother must be so proud of you," I tell her. With a humble confidence, she smiles and nods.

"Do you consider yourself an overachiever?" I ask. Sometimes after I've asked her a question, she takes a pause before responding, thinking through her words carefully.

"I attempt to put maximum effort into everything, which isn't always good," she answers. Still, balance to Kynnedy would look very different than what balance means to the average person. At her high school, she plays on the volleyball team, plays in the strings ensemble, and serves as a member of the speech and debate team, a founding member of the Black Student Union, and a member of the diversity club and the multicultural club. I am not sure how she juggles it all and maintains a 4.11 cumulative GPA. Kynnedy Simone Smith is a mastermind.

Now she is looking ahead to the future. "Yale, MIT, Stanford, Vanderbilt, Princeton," she says. "I have eighteen schools on my list."

Kynnedy wants to double-major in computer science and music performance. She's looking at colleges and universities that will allow her to explore art and technology. Eventually, she intends to set up a tech company that creates products catered to underrepresented communities. Academics, however, is not her only criterion for choosing a school.

"Right now, it's about fit," she explains. "Being a Black person, I have to think, how will it be as an African American woman there?"

Though she has been afforded many extraordinary opportunities, this is a question she has had to consider in almost all the spaces she has been in. However, her fit as a young Black woman was not in question when she was accepted and invited to attend the Disney Dreamers Academy in 2019. She calls the experience "one of the most life-changing things that ever happened." Kynnedy was chosen as one of one hundred distinguished teens to engage in the transformational and intensive four-day leadership program hosted by the Steve Harvey Foundation, *Essence* magazine, and Walt Disney World. "That was an environment that I know was meant for people like me," she reflects. "It was majority all Black people, and all of the presenters were Black and accomplished. Getting to hear from them and being able to present and perform in front of them gave me so much confidence. I realized that if I actually put in the work and I take advantage of this abundant community, then literally anything is possible. But then it also made me think, 'Why doesn't everyone have this experience?' That's when the mission for my organizations come in."

I Art Cleveland

"I started I Art Cleveland because art saved my life," Kynnedy says. "I'm not sure I would be here without art. Art created me into the leader I am today, and I want to use art in all fields to create other leaders."

Kynnedy was just eleven years old when she started her first nonprofit organization called I Art Cleveland. Its mission is to connect underrepresented youth in Northeast Ohio "to art education, programming, and funding sources," which are I Art Cleveland's three main initiatives. "There are thousands of kids in inner-city schools that don't have access to arts resources," Kynnedy says. "They don't have art or music. They just cut them off because of funding. If it wasn't for my arts classes, I would not have picked up a violin in the fourth grade."

The nonprofit provides community education about the importance of the arts and awareness about access to arts in the area. It also brings youth and partnering organizations together for both local and national arts experiences. Another I Art Cleveland endeavor has been to purchase tickets to various arts events, classes, and workshops and give them to families to encourage them to take in the arts in Cleveland. "We wanted people to appreciate art a bit more," Kynnedy says. "We try to incorporate 'art as healing.' Art is joy. We should be doing art because it makes us feel good."

Talking about I Art Cleveland is bittersweet for Kynnedy. She considers the organization one of her biggest successes, yet also a source of challenge and frustration. Kynnedy believes she was too young and inexperienced when she started I Art Cleveland. "You can't create big things by yourself," she says. "There was a lot more

I could have done with the organization if I really understood more about nonprofit management. I am learning more now."

Kynnedy is working on creating more initiatives and partnerships for I Art Cleveland and is optimistic that the organization is going in a new, more efficient direction. She even wants to expand it to have hubs in different cities. "This is my opportunity to rebrand I Art Cleveland and make it into something more. In ten years, it could be in at least thirty more cities."

I try not to downplay Kynnedy's moment of real frustration as she reflects, though I cannot help but be astonished at all she was able to accomplish at such a young age. "From my perspective, you have done so much," I reassure her. "I don't want for you to be too hard on yourself." She recounts that there was a point when she wanted to give up. And recently she came to a crossroads—a point of considering whether she should continue or discontinue the organization. Ultimately, she decided to stick it out. Kynnedy believed that it was important to push forward with what she had started despite the hurdles.

"This work needs to happen. Period. I can't just give up, because this is a real problem. I literally would not be who I am without arts. Think about all the people who are still trying to find themselves, who are lost and who don't have the resources that they need."

Chat(Her) Talks

After attending Disney Dreamers Academy, Kynnedy was inspired to start her second initiative, called Chat(Her) Talks, an online forum that gives all girls a seat at the table and creates a safe space for them to connect and inspire. Kynnedy started it to promote sisterhood and community; any person using the pronouns *she/*

her/hers or *they/them/their* can participate in Chat(Her). The Chat(Her) website describes the initiative as biweekly events that host speakers, including "youth who are effective leaders both locally and globally and who are a positive representation for their peers. They are advocates, authors, philanthropists, artists, STEMists, survivors, leaders, and most importantly they have a vital voice and investment in the positive development of women and girls."

Chat(Her) has covered topics on self-care, entrepreneurship, community leadership, college prep, politics, and STEM, just to name a few. A recent speaker series featured a discussion encouraging youth to become civic and community leaders in the wake of political and social unrest.

Kynnedy started Chat(Her) so she could share her community with others. "I didn't realize how many connections and resources I have had," she tells me. "I realized I had all these people in my network that have been helpful to me. Everyone needs to have this kind of community."

In Chat(Her) Kynnedy works with a team of other young Black women. All of them are accomplished teenagers and community leaders with a passion to empower and change the lives of other girls. She eventually wants to expand Chat(Her) to include mentoring, coaching, and a larger summit-style event. She is in the process of registering Chat(Her) as a 501(c)3 nonprofit. Like I Art Cleveland, she wants to expand Chat(Her) into a national and worldwide initiative. "I want to show girls that you can do anything you want to do at this age and be even more successful when you get older."

Kynnedy is intentional about her work. Her overall goal is to combine her interests in music, activism, arts, and STEM, an objective that is clear in all her organizational efforts. She sets high standards for herself and those who work alongside her. Kynnedy sets the pace, a distinct indication of the type of leader she has become.

The Balanced Pacesetter

Kynnedy's leadership style is that of a balanced pacesetter. The pacesetting leader sets the bar high. Leadership Ahoy!, a website that explores the various components of leadership, states that pacesetting occurs "when the leader sets an example of high performance, high pace, and high quality. . . . Team members watch the pacesetting leader and his or her speed, performance, and quality of work." The pacesetting leader is usually self-motivated, sets trends, takes initiative, and clearly communicates requirements. Kynnedy's leadership exhibits all these traits, and she has a strong desire for success and high quality. Though Kynnedy has high expectations for success and performance, she is willing to step aside and let others manifest their leadership: "I am in charge of everything as of right now, but as my team is growing, I have to make sure (1) that I have chosen the right people and (2) that I have inspired enough faith and been clear about the mission of the initiative that I can have confidence that my team is great and we are working together to create something bigger."

At times, pacesetting can be perceived as negative. When pacesetters' expectations are not met, such leaders may show little empathy for poor performers. Yet Kynnedy's naturally empathetic nature tempers her high expectations of others, allowing her to give more grace to those she works alongside.

If Kynnedy is hard on anyone, it's herself. When she reflects on some of the challenges in her organizations, she'll make statements like "I can't help but think I could have done more." Anything approaching failure feels unacceptable to a pacesetting leader. Such was the case, as we saw earlier, with Kynnedy's frustrations around I Art Cleveland. As a leadership style, pacesetting can be a great tool when managed properly. Kynnedy has to work hard to balance the high expectations she has for herself, which can sometimes lead to burnout or frustration.

Although pacesetting stands out within Kynnedy's leadership, she cannot be boxed into one style. Rather, she represents the best of a multiplicity of styles and frameworks that exemplify the unique layers of her gifts and talents. Pacesetting works best when other leadership styles emerge within the individual to provide balance. Kynnedy's strengths lie also in her capacity to be a visionary, a coach, and a strategist.

"You tell me something," she says, "and I think, 'Here are the possibilities that can happen. Here are the people that it can impact. Here's what we need to do to get there.'"

The Musical Genius of Ginger Smock

As we have seen, Kynnedy Simone (the name she goes by professionally) is a young Black woman, an arts activist, and a musician steeped in the arts community. She is part of a generational line of Black women who have held prominent roles in both the visual and the performing arts industries. Black women have impacted the art world through various mediums such as literature, music, cinema, architecture, and painting.

Unfortunately, Black women's art has historically been overlooked and marginalized by predominantly male and largely white arts movements. While there are many examples of unheralded artists of our past, the musical genius of jazz violinist Emma

"Ginger" Smock stands out. I watched a 1983 interview with Ginger Smock alongside Bette Yarbrough Cox for a series titled *Black Experience as Expressed through Music*. Like Kynnedy is, Ginger was easygoing and clever. She sat adjacent to the interviewer and was very poised. The conversation flowed effortlessly as though they had previously been acquainted. I felt like I was watching an older version of Kynnedy.

Born in Chicago in 1920, Smock demonstrated musical talent at a very young age. After her parents died, she was adopted by her aunt and uncle. Her aunt, who recognized her musical gift, bought Ginger her very first violin.

"She reared me and sacrificed everything. She did housework for an extra day so she could afford an extra violin lesson for me. That woman I owe everything to, to this day. She and her husband. I will never forget them for everything they've done for me," Ginger recounted.

By the time Ginger was ten years old, she was playing in large-scale venues like the Hollywood Bowl in California. "When I was a little girl, I'd listen on the radio to the Hot Club de France, and the leader was Stephon Grappeli, and he was a marvelous jazz violinist. He was my first inspiration," Smock said.

Through her teenage years, Smock continued to play in various spaces throughout Los Angeles and was a member of several distinguished musical organizations, including the LA Junior Philharmonic. By the time she became an adult, she had established herself as a prominent musician in the Los Angeles jazz scene. Her career continued to thrive as she made television appearances, worked as a studio musician, and traveled with multiple musical groups. She even played in churches throughout Los Angeles and later in Las Vegas, where she would reside. These churches were recognized not just as spiritual institutions but also as musical arts centers with many notable people playing on various occasions.

"Just playing for church," she said, "it's such a wonderful privilege and my way of saying 'Thank you God for giving me a gift.'"

Ginger Smock had an illustrious career despite continually facing limited opportunities because of her race and gender. Lamentably, those barriers also prevented her from gaining the widespread recognition she deserved. In "The Woman with the Violin," Steven Lewis writes about the struggles of Black women instrumentalists in those times: "The discrimination Smock struggled against throughout her career was representative of the obstacles facing black women instrumentalists in the mid-20th century. Although performing music was one of the few ways black women could move beyond a life of domestic or industrial labor, they often found themselves confined by the expectations and conventions of the male-dominated music industry. In their depictions of black female musicians, jazz promoters and writers often relied on stereotypes of 'exotic' black femininity that devalued and denigrated black women's musical skills."

Smock's love for the violin and for the arts in general compelled her to press forward despite these difficulties. She continued to perform, compose, and live out her God-given gifts without apology. In the article "Ginger Smock: First Lady of the Jazz Violin," author Laura Risk writes, "Her story may be punctuated with closed doors but is defined by those she pushed open and walked right through." Because Ginger continued to walk through those doors, young women like Kynnedy can walk through theirs.

Kynnedy's Leadership Wisdom

Kynnedy and the other young women in this book have inherited the same resilience of spirit and determination Ginger Smock embodied. The dimensions of Kynnedy's pacesetting leadership style are profound.

Take Things Step-by-Step

In our time together, Kynnedy shares many words of wisdom about life and leadership. Much of that wisdom comes from the audiobooks she listens to when she has some spare time. Her most recent audiobook is Anne Lamott's *Bird by Bird*, in which the author gives advice on writing and life. Based on a story from Lamott's life, in which her younger brother was overwhelmed by a school report in which he had to write about birds, the title of the book suggests the persistence that creativity requires. "Bird by bird, buddy," Lamott's father said. "Just take it bird by bird."

Focusing on one step at a time, and then the next, and then the next, is the lesson here. "All I have to do is to write down as much as I can see through a one-inch picture frame," Lamott writes. Kynnedy has written this quotation on a sticky note to remind herself to take things step-by-step, to stay within a framework she can manage, and to not overwhelm herself with tasks. This reminder resonates with Kynnedy as a high-achieving person. Too many possibilities can easily become overwhelming for her.

The idea of taking things step-by-step is an important notion for all of us. Whether faced with opportunities or obstacles, we can become overburdened by all we must do to get to our desired outcomes. Sometimes, however, the journey is as much about the road as it is about the destination. As an author, I find that people ask me as often about the *process* of writing a book as about the content. "How did you write all of that?" they ask. I think about that same question when I finally hold the book in my hand and reflect on the process it took to get here. The entire process is one sentence at a time, one paragraph at a time, and one chapter at a time. Like Kynnedy, I get overwhelmed if I muse too long about the magnitude of the process. My one-inch frame is just one chapter. Working within that frame means tackling just the next paragraph, even, before moving to the following task. I find this type of process helpful in many areas of my life.

There are lessons to be learned on the journey, and when we take things one step at a time, we can take advantage of all the teachable moments that come our way. Taking things step-by-step allows us to celebrate small wins instead of waiting for one big celebration at the end. What we want and need to accomplish will take time and patience.

Sisterhood Is Important

When I ask Kynnedy about her future goals and aspirations, I expect her to mention things like a career or a spouse or children. Although those may well be among her desires, she expresses a unique ambition: "In ten years? Personally, by then I want to make sure I have a community of sisterhood. Relationships are really important to me."

I don't usually hear this type of intention from young people. It wasn't until I was in my young adult years that I began to even understand the value that community and sisterhood add to my life. Kynnedy recognizes its value already, but she also realizes that this is an area she needs to grow toward.

"Being an only child, I didn't really know how to 'people,'" she tells me. By this she means that she didn't quite know how to socialize well. "I'm still learning how to 'people.' No one ever taught me. Most of my childhood was spent watching TV, reading books, or spending time with older people. I didn't know how to interact with people my age. Hopefully, by then [ten years from now], I would have found my people."

For young Black women who are often on the margins of society, Black sisterhood is important for identity and survival. Kelsey Adams, a Black woman who grew up in a white neighborhood in Toronto, always longed for a community of Black friends whom she would see as sisters. In her article "How Black Sisterhood Saved Me," she writes about feeling disconnected from Black sisterhood. When she was around other Black teens, she felt like she did not belong. She contemplates why this sisterhood is important, writing that Black women are a source of protection and escape. She feels solidarity and validation in their shared experiences of misogynoir—misogyny directed against Black women. "Black women give each other the confidence to survive a world that is inherently anti-Black and misogynistic," Adams writes. "Without this kind of empathetic support and care-taking, the world is a scary, isolating and sometimes violent place for us. So, it's no wonder we feel innately responsible for one another—we know that society wasn't built with us in mind, so we have to look out for each other."

Black women and girls need each other because we are crucial for our own survival. We need spaces where we can be our most authentic selves. We need spaces where we can nurture our hearts and souls with laughter, care, and understanding. Kynnedy understands that her success in this world is contingent upon her well-being. Part of that well-being emerges from the deep, emotional connection that comes with having a community of support and friendship. There is power in sisterhood.

We Can Learn from Our Failures

While Kynnedy is a very successful young woman, she speaks with me about her failures. She reflects on the areas she considered failures, not as a means of self-abasement, but to learn from those experiences and to better herself. She talks about what she considered failures with I Art Cleveland, but she has also channeled those experiences into teachable moments. In an interview Oprah did with hip-hop artist and entrepreneur Jay-Z, she stated, "So many people are afraid of failure, but what I've learned is that failure can be a great teacher, and if you're open to it, every mistake has a lesson to offer." Jay-Z responded in agreement: "I've learned more from failures than success. It can be paralyzing to some—failure and the fear of it."

As much as I hate failure, I must admit that, like Kynnedy, Oprah, and Jay-Z, I've found that failure has taught me some of life's greatest lessons. I recall once putting lots of time and energy into a major project, only to see the project not come to fruition. I was embarrassed and disappointed that it did not work out, and I felt like an all-around failure. I spent a great deal of time reflecting on what I had done wrong or what had gone awry. One day I heard a speaker ask: "What is this season teaching you right now?" In that moment, I realized that the failure contained lessons I could learn in order to make myself a better person. No one likes failure, but the lessons from failures often lead us to some of our greatest success.

The Hero of Her Own Story

In the middle of her senior year in high school, Kynnedy received some good news.

Dear Kynnedy,

Congratulations! Dean James J. Valentini and the members of the Committee on Admissions join me in the most rewarding part of my job—informing you that you have been admitted to the Columbia [University] Class of 2025.

"I've been working for this moment since I started school," she says with excitement.

Kynnedy was accepted to Columbia University on a full academic scholarship. She had applied to several colleges and universities, and Columbia was in her top seven. When she got in, she knew it was the school for her. Columbia offers a great mix of technology and the arts, and the fact that it is in New York City makes her believe that the school is perfect for her. She is still applying for scholarships for supplemental costs associated with going to college and so far has received scholarships and fellowships from organizations such as Coca-Cola and The Oprah Winfrey Charitable Foundation. Kynnedy does not want her mother to have to pay a dime for her college experience, and she has an entire spreadsheet of scholarships to apply for.

Kynnedy's mother is thrilled with her daughter's accomplishments. "It's definitely our collective win," Kynnedy says of the two of them. "The day after I got my acceptance letter, they sent my financial aid package and it said 'Parent contribution: $0.' [My mom] was so excited."

Kynnedy's ultimate goal is to make sure her family is financially stable and happy. Yet she is not "all work." She enjoys life too. "My senior year has been the most 'teenaged' of any year," she says. The past three years has been all grind, and it definitely paid off, but I feel like now I have a really solid friend group. We even had Friendsgiving. It was so lovely."

She beams talking about her friendships, and I can see that her long-term goal of having a close community of sisterhood has manifested itself much sooner than she'd imagined. "I believe in speaking things into the universe. I am really big on manifesting," she says, "manifesting power and peace for myself and my friends and family."

I can see that Kynnedy's commitment to daily affirmations, positive thinking, and hard work has resulted in rewards for her labor. At the same time, she knows that life is not formulaic. Life has its twists that we can neither control nor predict. Yet, even though we may not be in complete control, we can commit ourselves to trying our very best to get the most out of the lives that we have been blessed with. In a 2019 interview, Kynnedy was asked about the most essential lessons she learned through the Disney Dreamers Academy. She responded, "'Be the hero of your own story' is one of the statements that I think about just about every day. I have it written on my mirror in my room, and on my notebooks. It reminds me that I get to write this story and live out my journey, and it's up to me decide the happy ending."

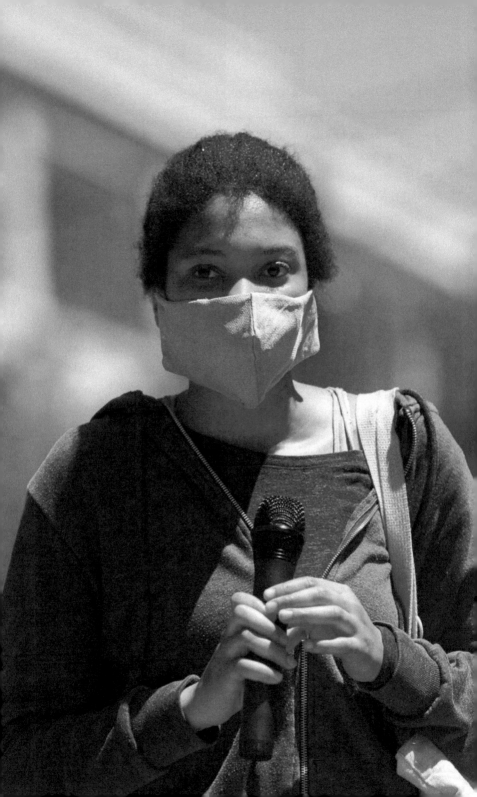

8

STANDING WITH THE PEOPLE
THE AGENCY OF STEPHANIE YOUNGER

When I was fourteen years old, my own experiences with misogynoir and the grief that comes from seeing police murdering Black people galvanized me into the work that I do.
–Stephanie Younger, founder of Black Feminist Collective

❧

Once upon a time, Stephanie Younger was too shy to speak in public. Often timid and withdrawn as a child, she never found that words flowed easily. Yet her sharp mind has always found a way to process the world through a critical lens.

It wasn't until she began working with the Richmond Youth Peace Project that she overcame her fear of public speaking. In response to police violence against Black people, Stephanie started performing spoken-word poetry. During one performance, she stood at the microphone in the center of the stage. Her tiny frame, her plain clothes, and her childlike face may have made the audience expect something simple or sweet. But that changed when they heard her poem, spoken in her quiet yet penetrating voice:

It is a crime to be Black.

It is a crime to have strong opinions.

To acknowledge the existence of racism.

It is a crime to be angry about the Black lives being ripped from their community.

Ignoring what we're born with and born into will not combat this.

Being Black is not a choice.

Stephanie's poem tells the story of an anonymous young Black person who gets stopped by an officer in a suburban neighborhood. She wrote the poem to channel her grief over police violence against Black people in the summer of 2016. When she wrote the poem, she imagined herself as the anonymous person. It's late at night, at a gas station, and the officer shoots them. She speaks directly to the victim: "Let your last words be 'Black Lives Matter. My life matters.'"

On any given day now, Stephanie Younger can be found at a rally, speaking boldly in front of crowds, protesting injustices, or silently holding various signs with poignant messages like:

Black girls are 6x more likely to be suspended.

Black youth have been combating violence for generations.

Listen to Black girls.

"According to my mom, she sang the Black National Anthem to me as I went to sleep [as a baby]. It's always been instilled in me to be pro-Black and to love my Blackness," Stephanie tells me.

Stephanie grew up in Virginia, the only child of two hard-working parents whom she loves to spend time with. She considers herself a creative who delves into protest art to address the intersection of racism and sexism. One of her latest mixed-media pieces was featured at the Virginia Museum of History and Culture. The featured piece was a silhouette of a Black Power fist wielded against a background of colorful sticky notes with handwritten statements listing her experiences and things people have said to her over the years:

"Why is it okay for Black kids to say the N-word?"

"Can we please not make this about race?"

"You have a good grade of hair."

"If you don't like this country, then get out."

Due to experiences of racism earlier in her life, Stephanie initially resented her Black identity. She says she internalized misogynoir from age six to twelve. Misogynoir is contempt directed toward Black women, and it is the word Stephanie uses often to describe what she has experienced. She has so many stories of traumatic racial incidents during her childhood and adolescence, especially within the school system in central Virginia. "I remember in pre-K, when I moved to Henrico, I was never invited to any of my classmates' parties," Stephanie recalls. "Never included. I never understood why." Typically, people do not have many memories from early childhood, but in Stephanie's case, her experiences were painful enough for her to recall almost every detail.

Stephanie experienced race-based trauma in school for most of her early adolescence as well. Racial trauma is an everyday reality for many Black children, who have been exposed to discrimination and bias. With that trauma comes psychological injury and stress. For Stephanie, these instances, which kept happening, brought about more emotional difficulty. "I remember my teacher often accused me of being physically aggressive toward other people," she says. "I remember being brought to the principal's office when I had a panic attack during a storm at school. I remember being accused of cheating for no reason. I remember these instances, but I never thought much of them until recently."

Like Amara Ifeji and me, Stephanie also experienced an incident of racism on the playground. One afternoon while she was playing on the monkey bars, a group of girls laughed and called her a monkey. After it happened, Stephanie told her mother, who spoke with her teacher about it. The teacher quickly excused the girls, saying, "Oh, no, we just read a book about monkeys, so it's okay."

"I had very few Black or brown classmates who were my friends," Stephanie added. "It was due to a lot of racism in the schools that I used to go to, and the racial trauma took a toll on my mental health. It's central Virginia. At one point they led the country in the school-to-prison pipeline, disproportionately affecting Black, brown, and disabled students."

Black Feminist Collective

The 2016 presidential election of Donald Trump ignited a women's movement. "I had just recently learned what feminism was," Stephanie recalls. "I actually learned what intersectionality was days after Trump was elected." *Intersectionality* is a term that describes the overlap of identities, like race and gender. In January 2017, she attended the women's march in Washington, DC, but she didn't quite understand her role as a Black person and a Black woman amid all the societal change.

While the early part of that year was the beginning of a personal exploration for Stephanie, it was the previous summer, in 2016, that changed the way she saw the world. The police shootings and subsequent deaths of Alton Sterling in Louisiana and Philando Castile in Minnesota led to protests all around the country. "Seeing the news coverage of Black people being murdered by the police, I was conflicted over what I should advocate for," Stephanie says. "Should I advocate for the collective liberation of my race, or should I advocate for the interests of the mainstream feminist movement?"

She came to the realization that she should not just advocate for the interests of Black men or white women, but also for Black women and girls. "Being Black and female is not mutually exclusive," she says. Wanting to center the work of Black women and girls, in May 2017 Stephanie penned an article that highlighted intersectionality. She created a website, posted the article, and within days, the post went viral. Tens of thousands of people were reading her words. She was only fourteen years old.

In it she wrote,

Many institutions fail to educate people about Black liberation and the feminist movement from the narratives [of] Black women, Black girls and Black non-binary people, who are often discredited for their work on the frontlines of Black liberation—which is often centered around cis[gender] het[erosexual] Black men, and mainstream

feminism—which often centers cishet white women. . . .
I am grateful [to] be part of a generation where Kimberle
Crenshaw's theory of intersectionality, Alice Walker's definition of womanism, and other movements led by Black
feminists are building a socially and politically just society.

She called the site where she posted the article "Black Feminist
Collective" and decided to use the attention to create a platform
for Black feminists—who often identify as womanists—to have a
voice. Black Feminist Collective has become an intergenerational
group that stands for Black liberation in its entirety and centers
the voices of Black feminists and womanists.

Black Feminist Collective currently has over sixty contrib-
uting authors who write about topics around Black liberation,
intersectionality, and womanism. These authors are not just from
the United States but also Latin America, Africa, and East Asia.
Stephanie has not only written opinion pieces but done interviews
with notable activists to highlight their work. Looking ahead, she
has begun wondering how to move this collective beyond writing
and virtual activism. She has been thinking about making Black
Feminist Collective into an organization.

Stephanie's personal activism has already extended beyond the
virtual platform as she has gotten more involved in community
organizing and training. "I went to nine protests this summer,"
she says with a grin that conveys self-confidence. She also tells me
about her work with the Richmond Youth Peace Project, "a youth
program of the Richmond Peace Education Center, emphasizing
conflict resolution, leadership training, peace, social justice and
positive self-expression through the arts." Stephanie was with the
project for three years and was trained in how to work with other

young people to apply nonviolent conflict resolution. "Even when I have conflicts with myself as a person, conflict resolution is a great tool for self-care and for de-escalation with other people."

Stephanie is an advocate for juvenile justice reform and gun violence prevention. She seeks to abolish, rather than reform, systems of imprisonment and policing. She has also continued to participate in and organize multiple rallies.

"Last month, a thirteen-year-old Black girl and I organized a protest that centered Black youth and encouraged the community to hear from us on the changes that we want to see in light of the police violence that's happening," she says. "There's a statue of Maggie Lena Walker in Richmond that was unveiled in 2017." Walker lived in post–Civil War Richmond and was known as a businesswoman and community leader. She was the first Black woman founder of a bank in the US. "We were intentional to host the protest there," Stephanie states, "because we wanted to remind the community that this fight for Black lives should center Black women."

Stephanie was overwhelmed by the support and turnout. About two hundred people showed up for the rally, and all the speakers were Black youth. "We had adults guiding us," she says, "but we were intentional that the young Black girls were leading the rally."

She is proudest of her involvement in the organization Rise for Youth, a nonpartisan campaign in support of community alternatives to youth incarceration. She has worked with this group for a couple of years now to dismantle the youth prison system. After someone connected with the organization saw one of Stephanie's spoken-word performances, she was invited to a screening of the documentary *Free Angela and All Political Prisoners*, about the social activism of political activist, academic, and author Angela Davis. There, Stephanie was inspired by Davis's work and even had an opportunity to meet and speak with her. That experience helped thrust Stephanie into advocacy for the abolition of prisons. "While seeing Angela Davis speak in person—and briefly meeting her—inspired me to learn more about abolition, it was my own experience with police, criminalization, and the grief that came from constantly seeing news coverage of state violence that thrust me into abolition work," she says.

Fighting and advocating for multiple causes can sound daunting and overwhelming, but to Stephanie, this lifestyle is normal for Black women: "People often forget that Black Lives Matter was started by three Black women. Three queer Black women. Black women led liberation movements. Black women leading the climate strikes. Fighting for gun violence. We've been doing this for generations."

Agency and Autonomy

Stephanie's early experiences of racial trauma made her feel powerless. She has since taken that power back, expressing it through her personal agency in her work. In the article "How Sociologists Define Human Agency," Dr. Nicki Lisa Cole writes that "agency refers to the thoughts and actions taken by people that express their individual power." Stephanie expresses her power through recognizing that she can influence her own thoughts and actions. She has taken agency over her own life and circumstances.

Stephanie embodies leadership through her organizing, her social media platforms, her writing, her art, and her speaking. The forces of patriarchy and racism have fused with the existing social structure throughout history, oppressing and exploiting women and people of color. This same social structure negatively affected Stephanie's well-being as a Black girl growing up in this society. Stephanie, however, has rejected that structure. She has every right to live as a free Black woman within this society and has dedicated her young life to freeing disenfranchised groups.

What emerges within Stephanie is a unique style of leadership known as autonomous leadership. In "Leadership Styles across Cultures," Caroline Osinski defines autonomous leadership as "independent and individualistic leadership attributes. Autonomous leaders emphasize individualism, independence and autonomy and have unique attributes."

This leadership style does not center only the autonomy of the leader but also the freedom the leader facilitates for those they work with. Stephanie is determined to elicit the same sense of freedom she has found from everyone she works with and for. This is also known as autonomy-supportive leadership. It fosters agency and allows individuals to take responsibility for their own actions. This kind of leadership not only enhances productivity; it inspires creativity and innovation as well.

Autonomous leaders like Stephanie set a clear mission and vision; they plan, set goals, and then get out of the way. For anyone who works alongside her, Stephanie is clear about her work's mission: the liberation of all Black people. As long as those she works alongside are on the same page with that mission, she allows space and freedom for them to create, plan, and write.

Black Liberation, Intersectionality, and Womanism

"When I was fourteen years old, my experiences with misogynoir and seeing news coverage of the police murdering Black people galvanized me," Stephanie reflects. "Seeing Angela Davis speak in person and hearing her story as an abolitionist, learning about other Black feminists like Kimberlé Crenshaw and Alice Walker inspired me to create Black Feminist Collective, organizing toward abolition and expressing myself through art."

Angela Davis, who helped to inspire Stephanie's prison advocacy, is most known for her work as an educator and political activist whose efforts have focused on race, class, feminism, and the prison abolition movement. She was an active member of several groups, including the Black Panther Party (the organization dissolved in 1982). In the early 1970s, Davis was wanted by the FBI in a case involving three Black prisoners and the shooting of a white guard. She was accused of purchasing weapons but was subsequently acquitted on all charges. Davis went on to have a prominent career as an academic, international speaker, organizer, and political activist.

Kimberlé Williams Crenshaw inspired Stephanie's commitment to intersectionality. Crenshaw is a prominent scholar who focuses her work on civil rights, Black feminist legal theory, and critical race theory. She is responsible for originating the word *intersectionality*, which is defined in the *Oxford English Dictionary* as "the interconnected nature of social categorizations such as race, class, and gender, regarded as creating overlapping and interdependent systems of discrimination or disadvantage; a theoretical approach based on such a premise." The term suggests that people are often oppressed according to multiple layers of their identity, which can include race, gender, sexual orientation, and other spheres. While Crenshaw is known for her work around intersectionality, her endeavors have extended to a variety of arenas. She is the executive director of the African American Policy Forum and a professor at Columbia Law School.

Just a few years before Crenshaw would coin the term *intersectionality*, writer, activist, and feminist Alice Walker gave us the word *womanism*. Walker noticed that the feminist movement focused primarily on white women and excluded injustices and discrimination that Black and brown women were experiencing. She created womanism as a distinction to describe Black feminists and other feminists of color. In many ways, Walker spoke to the intersectionality that Crenshaw would parse out later. Along with popularizing womanism, Walker has had an illustrious writing career, publishing numerous novels (including *The Color Purple*), poetry, essays, and scholarly work. She was a civil rights activist in the 1960s and has continued to speak out against injustice and discrimination both nationally and internationally throughout her career.

For Stephanie, Alice Walker's influence is the foundation of the Black Feminist Collective's published work. Influenced by these women activists, Stephanie moves the Black Feminist Collective forward on the principles of Black liberation, womanism, and intersectionality.

Stephanie's Leadership Wisdom

Stephanie believes that agency allows people room to learn and grow. She shared some of the important truths she has learned while finding her own voice and freedom.

Words Matter

Through her own liberation, Stephanie has become very intentional about the words she speaks. She is thoughtful about and conscious of how and when she uses her voice. At a young age, she understands that the words we use and how we use them matter greatly. Words had a tremendous effect on Stephanie as a child; her earlier painful experiences involved racist and misogynistic words spoken to her. As Stephanie shares with me stories of these encounters, she can recall almost every detail and how the words affected her psyche and her emotional well-being.

"Pre-K, kindergarten, first, second grade: they would bully me," Stephanie says. "They would talk about my hair. I internalized a lot of misogynoir, and I had to unlearn that."

Black girls experience these conflicting internal emotions at very young ages. They receive harmful messages about themselves and, in turn, internalize those stereotypes and negative words. In March 2020, a hairstylist named Shabria Redmond shared an Instagram video that went viral. In the video, a four-year-old named Ariyonna is looking into the camera while getting her hair done and says, "I'm so ugly." Shabria gasps in utter disbelief. "Don't say that!" she says to Ariyonna. "You are so pretty!" Ariyonna looks back at the camera and begins to cry. Shabria hugs and consoles Ariyonna while telling her, "You are a beautiful little girl. You are beautiful. Black is beautiful. And if don't nobody ever tell you, *I* will tell you. You are gorgeous, and you are going to grow up and be everything that you can be. Whatever you want to be."

The video is painful to watch because it's such a striking visual example of the internalized misogynoir that Stephanie talks about. Yet it's also a beautiful video, because viewers get to see Shabria countering the negative sentiments that Ariyonna feels with positive, encouraging words.

Stephanie has been there. I have been there. Somewhere along the line, four-year-old Ariyonna internalized the lie that her skin, her hair, and her personhood were ugly. I believe that not just negative imagery but detrimental words were the culprit. My own earliest painful experiences included words that caused me harm. At the same time, I can recall the time that I, like Ariyonna, first heard the phrase "Black is beautiful." Words like those seemed to erase the stigma associated with Blackness that I'd heard on the playground as a child.

For Stephanie, it was words like the following from Alice Walker that freed her from the poison of misogynoir. "Love yourself. Just love yourself," Walker says in an interview. "In fact, the love of the self cures every kind of problem you have with yourself. For instance, if someone calls you nappy-headed, it rolls right off your body if you love nappy hair. Or if someone calls you buck-toothed or too Black, that won't be a problem if you love being buck-toothed or Black. If you love it, then so what? The development of self-love cures many of the ills that people suffer from."

Create Your Own Platform

Novelist Toni Morrison once said, "If there's a book that you want to read, but it hasn't been written yet, then you must write it." Stephanie's activism is a living embodiment of that quotation. The Black Feminist Collective publication emerged because Stephanie had a message she wanted to get out. "I realized that Black cis [cisgender] men were often the face of liberation and white cis women were often the face of the feminist movement," she says. Stephanie then put pen to paper and wrote an article highlighting Black women, girls, and nonbinary people who are doing important womanist work in society. Stephanie needed a platform for her article. Instead of pitching her piece to an established site or media outlet, she created her own website and funneled the article through it. Stephanie created her own platform for her voice and, subsequently, for the voices of dozens of others committed to the work of liberation.

Many gifted and talented people wait for someone to come and provide them an opportunity to showcase their gifts. Such moments may or may not happen. What Stephanie knows and teaches us is that sometimes we must pave our own way. Sometimes we must create our own opportunities.

In a world that does not often give Black girls opportunities for their leadership to thrive, Black girls are paving the way. They are living examples of what it means to create their own platforms for success.

Stand Up for Others

Stephanie Younger is who I think of when I consider what true advocacy should look like. She has dedicated her life to speaking, writing, and standing up for marginalized people. Stephanie seizes any opportunity she can to be a voice alongside of and for others.

In the article "The Compassion Gene: Why Some People Are Born to Stand Up for Others," John Haltiwanger writes, "Some people are born with an inexplicable urge to help other people. There is something inside them that makes it unbearable to stand idly by while others suffer. These individuals are innately compassionate, altruistic, empathic and perpetually sensitive to the needs of others. They can barely fathom the cruel and violent history of this world but aren't ignorant to the sometimes sadistic tendencies of humanity." Stephanie is an advocate who stands up for and alongside others and does so with compassion and empathy.

Early in my career, I worked at a residential treatment facility for teenaged girls with severe emotional difficulties. The unit

I was assigned to had about ten girls ranging from thirteen to eighteen. Our job as residential counselors was to maintain a safe environment on the unit while monitoring the girls' behavior on each of our shifts.

One of the benefits of a girl's consistently good behavior was that she would be allowed to choose one of the staff as an advocate. An advocate would be assigned to a particular girl as her mentor; the advocate would also defend, support, and speak on the girl's behalf in meetings or other sessions where the girl was discussed. The advocate was the girl's ally when it came to all situations and circumstances.

After I'd worked on the unit for a few months, a girl named Danielle chose me as her advocate. Each time I came to work, she would excitedly scream, "Advocate!" Danielle would stick to my side like glue throughout my shift. She would brag to the other girls that her advocate was better than theirs. In meetings with adult staff, therapists, and nurses, I would make sure to speak on her behalf and ask for leniencies when appropriate. I sat in on her classes when she made presentations or in conferences with teachers when she needed an adult voice. I adored Danielle, and while I took my entire job seriously, I felt especially committed to my role as her advocate.

Years after I left that position, I came to realize that while I was there for all of the girls on that unit, God had put me there to stand with and on behalf of Danielle. I often reflect about the role I was given in her life and how I can translate that work to general advocacy efforts.

Stephanie's life and work are an example of that translation. "One of the biggest parts of being a leader, especially when it comes to activism and justice work, is to stand with people," she says. Stephanie knows what it is like to have no one standing up for her when she needed an advocate the most. Because of those experiences, as well as her passion for a free and just world, she can empathize with people who are most vulnerable. However, she doesn't consider herself a "voice for the voiceless," and she shuns that cliched phrase. Rather, Stephanie believes instead that "everyone has a voice that deserves to be uplifted."

We don't need to be born with extraordinary gifts or leadership traits to stand with people in need. Like Stephanie, we can use our platforms and spheres of influence to speak on behalf of and for the liberation of the oppressed.

Standing with the People

Stephanie Younger is a strong and resilient young Black woman. She is also gentle, sensitive, and vulnerable. She can embody all these traits: we need to learn to view all Black girls as full, three-dimensional humans.

"People have often called me a warrior," she says in her quiet tone. "I never thought much of it. I thought it was a compliment up until recently. Being called a warrior—it often leads people to believe that Black women don't feel pain. I am human. We're all human. Just because Black women have faced so much and risen in spite of that doesn't mean that we don't feel pain. We are deserving of comfort just as anyone else."

Stephanie's courageous activism does not erase the fact that her early adolescent experiences were riddled with racism and misogyny. She has since channeled these painful experiences into a mission to push back against oppression and be an agent for change. She says that her personal experiences, the experiences of her family, and the experiences of other Black women are what keep her going. Stephanie wants to dedicate her life to being an organizer and to use her skills to help communities. "I have always been a math and science person," she says, and her current major is computer science.

Stephanie says she is "just a young girl" who is still learning and growing. But she has come a long way from the meek and passive girl she once was, a girl who lived in the shadow of experiences of racial ignorance. She is no longer a powerless girl but, rather, a young woman who speaks and acts on her own behalf and moves through life with agency.

Stephanie will not stop until her mission is fulfilled: the liberation of Black people and justice for all who have been oppressed. A recent post on her Instagram page epitomizes her life's work: "The thing I reflected the most on in 2020 was learning that Black liberation looks like reclaiming our joy, by divesting from spaces that constantly show that they don't value us and rooting ourselves in self-care AND community care & creating spaces that center the liberation of all Black life (and that are not for white consumption) because we keep us safe at the end of the day."

Stephanie's life and work speak many messages, but the one that stands out the most to me is that we have the capacity to liberate ourselves.

CONCLUSION

██ If they don't give you a seat at the table, bring a folding chair," presidential candidate Shirley Chisholm once said. In some ways, that's what the young Black women featured in this book are doing: bringing their own folding chairs. The girls whose stories and leadership were shared here all have unique experiences, vary in age, and come from different backgrounds. What they share is their sheer will, desire, and passion to turn unfortunate circumstances into something hopeful. They use their influence and platforms to create and sustain social change and bring awareness to injustice. They use their God-given gifts to make the world a better place. Because of them I am more hopeful.

I am hopeful because somewhere in the smallest state in the country, there is a girl wanting to make the world a better place, and she is starting with the people right in her tiny community. I am hopeful because a seven-year-old girl who got a life-altering diagnosis decided to start an organization to put a smile on the faces of other kids to let them know they are not forgotten. I am hopeful because young girls across the country are marching for their rights and voices to be heard and taken seriously.

Along with these young women are countless Black girls leading the way in our nation and in this world. There's Marley Dias, the creator and founder of #1000BlackGirlBooks, "an international movement to collect and donate children's books that feature Black girls as the lead character." There is Naijai Graham-Henries, the world's youngest female barber. At only nine years old, she spends her time giving free haircuts to those in need. There's Mikaila Ulmer, who founded Me & the Bees Lemonade when she was just ten. Within two short years, the lemonade was being sold in more than five hundred stores, at the rate of 500,000 bottles a year. She donates a percentage of the profits to local and international organizations working to save honeybees.

These girls are human, and they have experienced life's joys and challenges like anyone else. Yet their resilience and imagination have compelled them to lead the way. They all give me hope for our future. I am hopeful because Black girls are shifting the narrative and taking their rightful seat at the table of leadership in the same manner that their foremothers did. The leadership of Black girls is multifaceted and resourceful. Black girls are transformational leaders, pacesetters, servant leaders, visionaries, mobilizers, ethical leaders, and more. There is much to be learned from the leadership practices of Black girls if we would just pay attention.

These girls do not claim to have all the answers, yet they feel confident that they can enact change with their resolve and determination. With their passion, they have confronted racial inequality and systemic injustice in their communities. They have moved forward with the confidence that they will be the generation to transform the world.

"This is the era when everything will change," Jaychele once said to me.

May we all sit back, watch, listen, and learn.

ACKNOWLEDGMENTS

S sanyu, Tyah, Hannah, Grace, Jaychele, Amara, Kynnedy, and Stephanie: Thank you. Thank you for taking the time to share your lives with me and for trusting me with your stories. You challenge me, you inspire me, and you give me so much hope for the future.

Mom and Dad, here I go again with another one of my ideas. And here you go again with your unfailing love and support. I can say the same for Shaun, my big brother, and of course my sister, Chloe, to whom this book is dedicated. I am so grateful to have a family that has always encouraged me and given me the confidence to be my very best.

Valerie Weaver-Zercher, God sent you to me. There's no way that an email you sent me in 2016 would come full circle the way it has without there being a divine purpose in mind. You helped me dream up *Parable of the Brown Girl*, and you helped me bring *Unbossed* to life. I am eternally grateful for you.

Elisabeth Ivey, your critical eye and challenging feedback alongside your grace were the perfect combination to give me the push I needed to tighten up this manuscript.

Portia Allen, you may not remember, but in the summer of 2020 during an interview on your podcast, I was mulling over who I was going to focus this book on. You reminded me that my heart is for Black girls: "Write about Black girls." You spoke a few words over my life. I remember them all.

And finally, to my friends, extended family, and community of support: As always, I am just a product of the love with which you have surrounded me.

NOTES

Introduction

4 *The importance of creating:* Lori Latrice Martin, *Black Women as Leaders: Challenging and Transforming Society* (Westport, CT: Praeger, 2019), 21.

Chapter 1

8 *I was so in love:* Unless otherwise noted, all quotes from Ssanyu Lukoma are from her conversation with the author, July/August 2020.

12 *The reason that #OwnVoices:* Alaina Leary, "30 Days of Social Justice," YALSA Blog, December 19, 2016, http://yalsa.ala.org/blog/2016/12/19/30-days-of-social-justice-why-the-ownvoices-movement-is-crucial-for-young-readers/.

14 *When I began to read Slay*: Ssanyu Lukoma, Review of *Slay*, Brown Kids Read, accessed June 23, 2021, https://brownkidsread.org/review/slay-by-brittney-morris-bkr-book-review/.

15 *I read about people:* Ssanyu Lukoma, "Our Founder," Brown Kids Read, accessed June 23, 2021, https://brownkidsread.org/about-brown-kids-read/.

15 *A manager's potential:* Prachi Juneja, "Strategic Leadership—Definition and Qualities of a Strategic Leader," Management Study Guide, accessed June 23, 2021, https://www.managementstudyguide.com/strategic-leadership.htm.

16 *Her innate strategic skills:* Richard L. Hughes, Katherine Colarelli Beatty, and David L. Dinwoodie, *Becoming a Strategic Leader: Your Role in Your Organization's Enduring Success, 2nd ed. (San Francisco: Wiley, 2014).*

16 *The 'obligation' to contribute:* Rosetta E. Ross, *Witnessingand Testifying: Black Women, Religion, and Civil Rights* (Minneapolis: Fortress, 2003), 4.

17 *(1) responsibility:* Ross, 11–12.

18 *DeLee worked to improve:* Ross, 117.

20 *Some advice I have:* Ellie McRae, "Interview with Ssanyu Lukoma," Kebloom, June 3, 2020, https://www.kebloom.com/inspiration/interview-with-ssanyu-lukoma.

Chapter 2

26 *I was calling my friends:* Unless otherwise noted, all quotes from Tyah-Amoy Roberts are from her conversation with the author, July/August 2020.

28 *I am here today:* "Black Parkland Survivors Want to be Heard." CNN, n.d. https://www.cnn.com/videos/us/2018/03/29/parkland-school-black-students-orig-llr.cnn

30 *To convening:* "About USOW," Civic Nation, 2021, https://usow.org.

32 *Enacted in its authentic form:* Nancy C. Roberts, "Transforming Leadership: A Process of Collective Action," *Human Relations* 38, no. 11 (November 1985): 1023–46.

32 *Burns referred to this kind of leadership:* J. M. Burns, *Leadership* (New York: Harper & Row, 2010).

32 *In her book Transformative Leadership:* Carolyn M. Shields, *Transformative Leadership: A Reader* (New York: Peter Lang, 2011), 1–17.

34 *A rich history:* Yvette Lynne Bonaparte, "A Perspective on Transformative Leadership and African American Women in History," *The Journal of Values-Based Leadership* 8, no. 2 (Summer-Fall 2015): 5.

35 *If I'm elected:* "Fannie Lou Hamer's Powerful Testimony," *American Experience*, PBS, June 23, 2014, https://www.youtube.com/watch?v=07PwNVCZCcY&feature=emb_title.

35 *Hamer was blunt:* Breanna K. Barber, "Tell It on the Mountain: Fannie Lou Hamer's Pastoral and Prophetic Styles of Leadership as Acts of Public Prayer" (undergraduate thesis, University of Montana, 2015), 7, https://scholarworks.umt.edu/cgi/viewcontent.cgi?article=1033&context=utpp.

35 *There is so much hypocrisy:* Fannie Lou Hamer and Jack O'Dell, "Oral History/Interview, Life in Mississippi," *Freedomways*, Spring 1965, https://www.crmvet.org/nars/flh1.htm.

37 *The self that God* David G. Benner, *The Gift of Being Yourself* (Downers Grove, IL: InterVarsity, 2015), 61.

40 *I wrote about this topic:* Khristi Lauren Adams, *Parable of the Brown Girl: The Sacred Lives of Girls of Color* (Minneapolis: Fortress, 2020), 18.

40 *Caring for myself:* Audre Lorde, *A Burst of Light and Other Essays* (Mineola, NY: Ixia, 2017), 130.

41 *Time magazine found:* Chris Wilson, "This Chart Shows the Number of School Shooting Victims since Sandy Hook," *Time*, Feburary 22, 2018, https://time.com/5168272/how-many-school-shootings/.

Chapter 3

45 *Chapter 3 note:* This chapter explores the theme of suicide, which some may find distressing.

46 *I ran over to her:* "After a Suicide Attempt, This Teen Created an App to [Help] Others Struggling with Mental Health Issues," Facebook Watch video, 4:18, Stitch, October 16, 2020, quote at 1:56, https://www.facebook.com/watch/?v=633895867295327.

46 *No one thought:* Unless otherwise noted, all quotes from Hannah Lucas are from her conversation with the author, July/August 2020.

47 *What if all Black women:* Black Women's Health Imperative, 2021, https://bwhi.org/.

49 *One of the girls I interviewed:* Khristi Lauren Adams, *Parable of the Brown Girl: The Sacred Lives of Girls of Color* (Minneapolis: Fortress, 2020), 23.

49 *I felt out of control:* Adams, 23.

49 *Suicide attempts increased:* Katelyn Newman, "Suicide Attempt Rates for Black Teens Continue to Rise," *US News & World Report*, October 19, 2019, https://www.usnews.com/news/healthiest-communities/articles/2019-10-14/study-suicide-attempt-rates-for-black-teens-continue-to-rise.

50 *I witnessed her:* "After a Suicide Attempt," 1:35.

50 *According to one survey:* "Americans Check Their Phones 96 Times a Day," Asurion, November 21, 2019, https://www.asurion.com/about/press-releases/americans-check-their-phones-96-times-a-day/#:~:text=Americans%20now%20check%20their%20phones,tech%20care%20company%20Asurion1.

Notes

50 *Other survey data:* "30 Truly Fascinating App Usage Statistics to Know in 2021," WebsiteBuilder, March 20, 2021, https://websitebuilder.org/blog/app-usage-statistics/#:~:text=16.,1%E2%80%9310%20times%20per%20day.&text=Recent%20surveys%20and%20mobile%20app,times%20in%20a%20single%20day.

53 *Other users have written:* Reviews quoted here are visible via iPhone or iPad on the notOK app page at the Apple app store; https://apps.apple.com/us/app/notok/id1322629109.

53 *In their article Frances:* Westley and Henry Mintzberg, "Visionary Leadership and Strategic Management," in Strategic Leaders and Leadership, special issue, *Strategic Management Journal* 10 (Summer 1989): 17–32, http://www.wiggo.com/mgmt8510/readings/readings11/westley1989smj.pdf

53 *What distinguishes:* Westley and Mintzberg, 19.

54 *Vision is our view:* Randy Grieser, "The Importance of Visionary Leadership," Achieve Centre for Leadership and Workplace Performance, accessed July 8, 2021, https://ca.achievecentre.com/blog/importance-visionary-leadership/.

55 *Vision for the creator:* Westley and Mintzberg, "Visionary Leadership," 24.

55 *Vision is often experienced:* Westley and Mintzberg, 24.

56 *Harriet Tubman, known as:* Jean M. Humez, "In Search of Harriet Tubman's Spiritual Autobiography," *National Women's Studies Association Journal* 5, no. 2 (Summer 1993): 162–82.

56 *She did have visions:* Karu F. Daniels, "Harriet Tubman's Descendant Tells *Daily News* New Movie on Abolitionist Is Long Overdue—and It's Good!," *New York Daily News*, November 1, 2019, https://www.nydailynews.com/snyde/ny-harriet-tubman-movie-descendant-ernestine-martin-debra-martin-chase-20191101-c3r4reuylrbhpphanunxdmap3u-story.html.

57 *Based on her research:* Liz Beck, "Why Harriet Tubman's Spirituality and Premonitions Were Essential to the New Biopic," *Bustle*, October 23, 2019, https://www.bustle.com/p/harriet-tubmans-visions-from-god-play-a-major-role-in-the-new-biopic-19251946.

59 *God prescribed:* Rick Warren, *The Purpose Driven Life: What on Earth Am I Here For?* (Grand Rapids: Zondervan, 2013), 26.

60 *One of the best guides:* bell hooks, *All About Love: New Visions* (New York: William Morrow, 2018), 67–68.

60 *The December 2020 article:* Teen Vogue Staff, "*Teen Vogue's* 21 Under 21, 2020: The Girls and Femmes Building a Better Future," Teen Vogue (November 24, 2020), https://www.msn.com/en-us/lifestyle/lifestyle-buzz/teen-vogues-21-under-21-2020-the-girls-and-femmes-building-a-better-future/ar-BB1bj9Si.

60 *In the same month:* Jada Pinkett Smith, "Suicide Attempt Survivors Speak Out," Red Table Talk (video, 35:51), Facebook Watch, December 22, 2020, https://www.facebook.com/watch/?v=2479559695672480.

Chapter 4

66 *She thought I had braided:* Unless otherwise noted, all quotes from T'Jae Ellis are from her conversation with the author, July/August 2020.

68 *Further complicating matters:* Nataki Douglas, "I'm a Doctor, and I Want to Talk about the Racial Disparities That Affect Black Women's Health," Well+Good, February 28, 2020, https://www.wellandgood.com/black-women-health-care/.

68 *Callwood:* Unless otherwise noted, all quotes from Grace Callwood are from her conversation with the author, July/August 2020.

71 *Bring happiness:* The We Cancerve Movement, Inc., accessed July 9, 2021, https://www.wecancerve.org/about-us-1.

71 *The We Cancerve Movement:* "Our Projects," The We Cancerve Movement, Inc., accessed July 9, 2021, https://www.wecancerve.org/upcomingevents.

72 *In a 2009 interview:* Desmond Tutu on Leaders as Servants," *The BLG Blog*, Bacharach Leadership Group, May 27, 2009, http://blg-lead.com/desmond-tutu-on-leaders-as-servants.

72 *Servant leadership:* Robert K. Greenleaf, *The Servant as Leader*, 6, http://www.ediguys.net/Robert_K_Greenleaf_The_Servant_as_Leader.pdf.

72 *They hear things:* Greenleaf, 24.

72 *Based on Greenleaf's definition:* Larry Spears, "Ten Characteristics of a Servant Leader," The Spears Center for Servant-Leadership, November 1, 2018, https://www.spearscenter.org/46-uncategorised/136-ten-characteristics-of-servant-leadership.

74 *Servant leadership has been in practice:* Debora Y. Fonteneau and Brenda L. H. Marina, "Servant Leaders Who Picked Up the Broken Glass," *The Journal of Pan African Studies* 5, no. 2 (April 2012): 72.

74 *These women didn't stand:* Janet Dewart Bell, "The Selfless Servant Leadership of the African-American Women of the Civil-Rights Movement," *The Nation*, April 25, 2018, https://www.thenation.com/article/archive/the-selfless-servant-leadership-of-the-african-american-women-of-the-civil-rights-movement/.

75 *I will not allow:* Paris Alston, "Boston Globe Columnist Illustrates the 'Beautiful Resistance' in Black Life." Wbur, December 8, 2020, https://www.wbur.org/radioboston/2020/12/08/jenee-osterheldt-beautiful-resistance.

77 *In her article:* Ingrid Fetell Lee, "Joy Is an Act of Resistance: How Celebration Sustains Activism," The Aesthetics of Joy, November 8, 2019, https://aestheticsofjoy.com/2019/11/08/joy-is-an-act-of-resistance-how-celebration-sustains-activism-2/.

78 *Leadership:* "Theory and Practice," 7th ed. (Los Angeles: SAGE Publications, 2016), 228.

78 *Imagine lying on a beach:* "Beach in a Bucket," We Cancerve Movement, Inc., accessed July 9, 2021, https://www.wecancerve.org/beach-in-a-bucket.

78 *Chemo treatments:* "Books & Buddies," We Cancerve Movement, Inc., accessed July 9, 2021, https://www.wecancerve.org/books-buddies.

79 *Finding [an Easter] basket:* "Eggstra Special Easter 'Bagskits,'" We Cancerve Movement, Inc., accessed July 9, 2021, https://www.wecancerve.org/eggstra-special-easter.

79 *How can wounds:* Henri Nouwen, *The Wounded Healer* (New York: Image, 1979), 94.

79 *Hospitality is the virtue*: Nouwen, 95.

Chapter 5

86 *We just said:* Unless otherwise noted, all quotes from Jaychele Nicole Schenck are from her conversation with the author, July/August 2020.

86 *The youth are fed up:* "Gen Z We Want to Live Press Conference," YouTube video, 3:43, Uprise RI, June 12, 2020, quote at 2:14, https://www.youtube.com/watch?time_continue=153&v=QhCvI-mFvqg&feature=emb_logo.

86 *People are:* "2020-06-14 Gen Z We Want to Live 01 Burnside Park," YouTube video, 7:34, Uprise RI, June 14, 2020, quote at 1:50, https://www.youtube.com/watch?v=DPnTJaFB82U&t=111s.

87 *Through youth advocacy:* Gen Z: We Want to Live, website, https://www.genzwwtl.org/.

87 *I've noticed that:* Ryan Brooks, "Generation Free Fall," BuzzFeed News, April 20, 2020, https://www. buzzfeednews.com/article/ryancbrooks/gen-z-young-millennials-coronavirus-pandemic-recession?bftwnews&utm_term=4ldqpgc#4ldqpgc.

91 *As a youth:* "Jaychele Schenck: Gun Control from the Perspective of a Youth Activist, a Poem," Uprise RI, June 3, 2019, https://upriseri.com/2019-06-03-jaychele-schenck/.

92 *Engage in activities:* Peter G. Northouse, *Leadership: Theory and Practice* (New York: SAGE, 2018), 258.

93 *Adaptive leadership:* Kevin McDermott, Barry Colbert, and Elizabeth Kurucz, "Mobilizing Leadership: Leading Cross-Sector Partnerships as a Social Movement," The Intersector Project, November 28, 2017, http://intersector.com/researcher-insights-mobilizing-leadership-leading-cross-sector-partnerships-as-a-social-movement/.

93 *Similar to a physician*: Northouse, *Leadership*, 260.

94 *Black women who are engaged*: Lori Latrice Martin, *Black Women as Leaders: Challenging and Transforming Society* (Westport, CT: Praeger, 2019), 1.

95 *Thank you:* Kamala Harris (@KamalaHarris), Twitter, November 9, 2020, 2:32 p.m., https://twitter.com/kamalaharris/status/1325898963153805312?lang=en.

96 *I'm not going to tell you:* "Jaychele Schenck," https://upriseri.com/2019-06-03-jaychele-schenck/.

97 *It is my truth:* "Activist Tamika Mallory on Policing & Patrolling, White Aggression in America, Being A Leader + More," *Nick Cannon Mornings*, YouTube video, 34:40, Power 106 Los Angeles, July 8, 2020, quote at 12:29, https://www.youtube.com/watch?v=azsQFxB9t5s.

98 *While on tour:* Heard by the author in Philadelphia in 2018, but also documented here: Maura Hohman, "Michelle Obama Tells

Oprah Why She 'Sobbed for 30 Minutes' after Leaving the White House," People, November 14, 2018, https://people.com/politics/michelle-obama-oprah-sobbed-leaving-white-house/.

98 *Your True Nature*: Aletheia Luna, "Higher Self: 11 Ways to Connect with Your Soul," Lonerwolf, July 10, 2021, https://lonerwolf.com/higher-self/.

Chapter 6

103 *I started off exploring*: Unless otherwise noted, all quotes from Amara Ifeji are from her conversation with the author, July/August 2020.

104 *As she graduates:* Bill Nemitz, "Changing the World, One Small Corner at a Time," Portland Press Herald, June 7, 2020, https://www.pressherald.com/2020/06/07/bill-nemitz-changing-the-world-one-small-corner-at-a-time/.

104 *In Maine's schools*: Laura Fralich, "The Confederate Flag and a Legacy of Racism in Maine," *Bangor Daily News*, July 7, 2020, https://bangordailynews.com/2020/07/07/opinion/contributors/the-confederate-flag-and-a-legacy-of-racism-in-maine/.

105 *In Maine there are many:* Ryan Caron King, "Why Young Protesters Are Fighting for Racial Justice in New England," video, 10:47, Connecticut Public Radio, September 16, 2020, quote at 1:37, https://www.ctpublic.org/news/2020-09-16/video-why-young-protesters-are-fighting-for-racial-justice-in-new-england.

110 *Environmental equity*: "Environmental Equity vs. Environmental Justice: What's the Difference?" Mobilize Green, September 30, 2018, https://www.mobilizegreen.org/blog/2018/9/30/environmental-equity-vs-environmental-justice-whats-the-difference.

111 *Historically, the environmental debate:* Vanessa Fabien, "African American Environmental Ethics: Black Intellectual Perspectives 1850–1965," dissertation, University of Massachusetts Amherst, November 2014, https://scholarworks.umass.edu/cgi/viewcontent.cgi?article=1210&context=dissertations_2.

113 *A youth-led intergenerational network:* "Program Overview," Maine Environmental Changemakers Network, accessed July 10, 2021, https://www.meeassociation.org/programs/changemakers.

Notes

113 *The African American community:* Heber Brown III, in Amy Frykholm, "The Black Church Food Security Network Aims to Heal the Land and Heal the Soul," *The Christian Century*, November 10, 2020, https://www.christiancentury.org/article/interview/black-church-food-security-network-aims-heal-land-and-heal-soul.

114 *My first time going there:* Irwin Gratz, "Maine Student Named National Geographic Young Explorer for Environmental Work," Main Public Radio, February 5, 2021, https://www.mainepublic.org/post/maine-student-named-national-geographic-young-explorer-environmental-work.

114 *Many nights I just sit:* "An American Beach," YouTube, January 28, 2007, https://www.youtube.com/watch?v=-D2lPKbDliY&feature=emb_title.

116 *In Leadership:* Peter G. Northouse, *Leadership: Theory and Practice* (New York: SAGE, 2018), 341–346.

116 *Amara's ethical code* "Future Focus with Amara Ifeji," YouTube video, 35:02, Maine Audobon Media, December 1, 2020, quote at 27:03, https://www.youtube.com/watch?v=fUilRnQHvl4&list=UUGPr9ko8mc3aIyK6rYKt72g.

116 *We cannot transform*: Otto Scharmer and Karin Kaufer, *Leading from the Emerging Future: From Ego-System to Eco-System Economies* (Oakland, CA: Berrett-Koehler, 2013), 19.

116 *If you have come:* "The Origin of 'Our Liberty Is Bound Together,'" Invisible Children, accessed August 8, 2021, https://invisiblechildren.com/blog/2012/04/04/the-origin-of-our-liberty-is-bound-together/.

117 *Skillful judgment:* Dictionary.com, s.v. "critical," accessed July 10, 2021, https://www.dictionary.com/browse/critical.

117 *A social theory:* Ashley Crossman, "Understanding Critical Theory," ThoughtCo., October 15, 2019, https://www.thoughtco.com/critical-theory-3026623.

119 *In her article:* M. B. Hewitt, "Helping Students Feel Like They Belong," *Reclaiming Children and Youth 7*, no. 3 (1998): 155–59.

119 *Looking back to her interview:* "Future Focus with Amara Ifeji."

121 *Changing the world*: Nemitz, "Changing the World."

Chapter 7

126 *My mom really worked hard:* Unless otherwise noted, all quotes from
Kynnedy Simone Smith are from her conversation with the author, July/
August 2020.

127 *My mother listened:*" Yolanda Baruch, "Disney Dreamer Talks Dreamers
Academy and Landing Mentorship with Richelieu Dennis, Ower of
Essence Magazine," Lee Bailey's *EurWeb*, October 30, 2019,
https://eurweb.com/2019/10/30/disney-dreamer-talks-dreamers-
academy-and-landing-mentorship-with-richelieu-dennis-owner-of-
essence-magazine/.

129 *Kynnedy was just eleven:* "About," I Art Cleveland website, accessed July
11, 2021, https://www.iartcleveland.org/about.

131 *Youth who are effective leaders:* Chat(Her) Talks website, accessed July 11,
2021, https://www.chathertalks.com/.

132 *When the leader:* Carl Lindberg, "Pacesetting Leadership: What Is It?
Pros/Cons? Examples?," Leadership Ahoy!, accessed August 8,
2021, https://www.leadershipahoy.com/pacesetting-leadership-
what-is-it-pros-cons-examples/.

134 *I watched a 1983 interview:* "Ginger Smock Interviewed by Bette
Yarbrough Cox," video, 41:28, *Black Experience as Expressed through Music*,
California Revealed, February 24, 1983, https://californiarevealed.org/
islandora/object/cavpp%3A17992.

134 *She reared me*: "Ginger Smock," 27:55.

134 *When I was a little girl:* "Ginger Smock," 7:50.

135 *The discrimination:* "The Woman with the Violin: Ginger Smock and the
Los Angeles Jazz Scene," National Museum of African American History
and Culture, January 11, 2019, https://nmaahc.si.edu/explore/stories/
collection/Ginger-Smock.

135 *Her story:* Laura Risk, "Ginger Smock: First Lady of the Jazz Violin,"
Strings, October 30, 2020, https://stringsmagazine.com/ginger-smock-
first-lady-of-the-jazz-violin.

136 *Bird by bird:* Anne Lamott, Bird by *Bird: Some Instructions on Writing and
Life*, 2nd Anchor Books ed. (New York: Penguin Random House, 2019), 18.

136 *All I have to do:* Lamott, 64.

138 ***Black women give each other***: Kelsey Adams, "How Black Sisterhood Saved Me," Flare, May 31, 2020, https://www.flare.com/identity/black-female-friendships/.

139 ***So many people are afraid***: "Oprah's Master Class: Jay Z," OWN, January 1, 2011, YouTube video (audio only), 31:40, posted April 26, 2021, quote at 12:47, https://www.youtube.com/watch?v=MNQH-Kxwx7E.

141 ***'Be the hero of your own story'***: Baruch, "Disney Dreamer."

Chapter 8

143 ***It is a crime to be Black***: Stephanie Younger, "Does My Life Matter (original poem)," YouTube video, 1:50, Generation Dream 2017, Richmond Peace Education Center, February, 15, 2017; video uploaded March 30, 2017, https://www.youtube.com/watch?v=PS4XwaQSWI0.

145 ***According to my mom***: Unless otherwise noted, all quotes from Stephanie Younger are from her conversation with the author, July/August 2020.

148 ***Many institutions fail***: Stephanie Younger, "14 Black Girls, Women & Non-Binary People Every Intersectional Feminist Should Know About," Black Feminist Collective, May 5, 2017, https://blackfeministcollective.com/2017/05/05/14-black-women-girls-and-nonbinary-people-every-intersectional-feminist-should-know-about/.

148 ***A youth program***: Richmond Youth Peace Project Facebook Post, accessed July 11, 2021, https://www.facebook.com/Richmond-Youth-Peace-Project-RYPP-287265678046496/.

149 ***She is proudest***: Rise for Youth website, accessed July 11, 2021, https://www.riseforyouth.org/.

150 ***Agency refers to the thoughts***: Nicki Lisa Cole, "How Sociologists Define Human Agency," ThoughtCo., January 2, 2021, thoughtco.com/agency-definition-3026036.

151 ***Independent and individualistic***: Caroline Osinski, "Leadership Styles across Cultures," HR Exchange, February 21, 2014, https://www.hrexchangenetwork.com/learning/articles/leadership-styles-across-cultures#:~:text=Autonomous%3A%20Autonomous%20leadership%20refers%20to,autonomy%20and%20have%20unique%20attributes.

153 *Influenced by:* "About," Black Feminist Collective website, https:// blackfeministcollective.com/about/.

154 *In the video:* wediditjoe.ig, "We Must UPLIFT Our Queens," Instagram post and video, March 5, 2020, https://www.instagram.com/tv/ B9Xr7P7lhxh/?utm_source=ig_embed&ig_rid=647d7c25-cff3-49ac-a05f-73505380f4e9

155 *Alice Walker:* The 'PBS American Masters' Interview," African American Literature Book Club, February 1, 2014, https://aalbc.com/interviews/ interview.php?id=51.

155 *If there's a book:* Associated Press, "Toni Morrison's Most Notable Quotes about Life, Race and Storytelling," USA Today, August 7, 2019, https:// www.usatoday.com/story/entertainment/books/2019/08/07/toni-morrison-nobel-prize-winning-writer-most-notable-quotes/1941628001/.

156 *John Haltiwanger:* "The Compassion Gene: Why Some People Are Born to Stand Up for Others," Elite Daily, September 10, 2015, https://www. elitedaily.com/life/compassion-gene-why-people-born-stand-up-others/1206696.

Conclusion

162 *An international movement:* "About Me," Marley Dias website, accessed July 11, 2021, https://www.marleydias.com/about/.